Georg Ossian Sars

On Some Remarkable Forms of Animal Life From the Great

Deeps off the Norwegian Coast

Georg Ossian Sars

**On Some Remarkable Forms of Animal Life From the Great Deeps off the
Norwegian Coast**

ISBN/EAN: 9783337242909

Printed in Europe, USA, Canada, Australia, Japan

Cover: Foto ©Andreas Hilbeck / pixelio.de

More available books at **www.hansebooks.com**

ON

SOME REMARKABLE FORMS OF ANIMAL LIFE

FROM THE GREAT DEEPS OFF THE NORWEGIAN COAST.

(SEQUEL TO THE UNIVERSITY PROGRAM PUBLISHED UNDER THE SAME TITLE IN 1872; PARTLY FROM
POSTHUMOUS MANUSCRIPTS OF THE LATE PROFESSOR Dr. M. SARS),

II.

RESEARCHES ON THE STRUCTURE AND AFFINITY OF THE GENUS

BRISINGA,

BASED ON THE STUDY OF A NEW SPECIES:

BRISINGA CORONATA.

BY

GEORGE OSSIAN SARS,

PROFESSOR OF ZOOLOGY AT THE UNIVERSITY OF CHRISTIANIA.

WITH 4 COPPER PLATES AND 3 AUTOGRAPHIC PLATES.

University-Program for the last half-year 1875.

CHRISTIANIA.

1875.

CONTENTS.

I.

Introduction.

In the year 1853 Mr. P. Chr. Asbjornsen, the celebrated Norwegian poet and naturalist, was dredging in the picturesque Hardangerfjord, and obtained here from the great depth of 200 fathoms a very remarkable star-like Echinoderm quite unlike all that had hitherto been known. Owing to its highly magnificent appearance, and in the presentiment of its true relation to forms long ago extinct, he applied to it the very characteristic and excellent mythological appellation *Brisinga* [1]), derived from „Brising", the breast-ornament of Freya, which according to ancient Norwegian tradition was concealed by Loke in the abyss of the primitive Ocean. In 1856 he announced his important discovery in the 2ᵈ Vol. of Fauna littoralis Norvegiæ, where the animal in question was briefly described as a new genus and species of Asteridæ under the denomination of *Brisinga endecacnemos*.

Among the forms of animal life discovered in recent times there are indeed few so highly interesting as this remarkable Star-fish, distinguished alike by its extremely peculiar exterior and brilliant color and by its gigantic size. It exhibits in reality an appearance so totally different from that of all hitherto known forms, that we cannot be surprised, that the authors have been, and still are, in great doubt as to what place in the system it should properly occupy. According to its external form we might be inclined to refer it to the group of Brittle-stars or Ophiuræ with which it seems specially to agree in its small circular disc and the enormously prolonged arms or rays issuing from the same; while on the other hand there are important features (such as the deep and wide ambulacral furrows running

[1] With reference to this name the learned Italian professor Sgn. *Angelo de Gubernatis* says in the 2ᵈ Vol. of his „Mythologie zoologique" pg. 453: . . . . „En effet, soit qu'on les (les mythes) examine en détail, soit qu'on les prenne dans leur ensemble, on est obligé de convenir que le ciel est le grand miroir, dans lequel se sont reflétées toutes les images primitives du langage humain. Ce n'est pas par hasard que le célèbre conteur et naturaliste Norwégien, P. Chr. Asbjørnsen, a donné le nom mythologique de *Brisinga* à une nouvelle espèce d'animal découverte par lui au fond de la mer du Nord, et offrant une ressemblance frappante par sa conformation avec le soleil, la perle lumineuse, l'anneau magique, qui tombe dans l'eau et que retrouve le poisson mythique. Il n'y a que les poètes qui soient capables de deviner, de saisir l'instinct certaines vérités de la science, et Asbjørnsen est un grand poète."

1

along the under-side of the arms, with their 2 rows of strongly developed water-feet or tentacles, the presence of a dorsal madreporic body and of numerous pedicellariæ) which tell decidedly against such an annexation, and point rather to the proper star-fishes (Asteriæ) for which reason my Father* also has expressed himself decidedly of opinion that in spite of its different appearance it ought to be referred to the latter order. Nevertheless the opinions as to the systematic place of this form seem still to be much divided; and Bronn[1] and also in later times Haeckel[2] have therefore seen no other expedient than to establish for it an entirely new order. *Brisingastra:* as in the opinion of these naturalists it seems too peculiar to be incorporated in any of the orders previously established in the class of Asteroidea. At present therefore this remarkable genus stands completely isolated, without connexion with the forms hitherto known; and even the fossile form *Protaster,* which is considered by Asbjörnsen as its nearest relative, exhibits in many essential points considerable divergences, agreeing in its general aspect much more closely with the normal star-fishes. A more exhaustive investigation of this remarkable form than that given by Asbjörnsen in his preliminary description, must therefore certainly be highly interesting; and has also probably been long desired and expected by the scientific world, in order that more light may be thrown on the morphology of this highly enigmatic form; and on its relation to the other Asteroidea. The great rarity of the species first discovered, and its very limited occurrence, only on one single secluded spot in the deep Hardangerfjord, where the use of the dredge is connected with no small difficulty, has however as yet placed insuperable obstacles in the way of such investigation, for which abundant material is above all things absolutely requisite. Every specimen occasionally taken up has been regarded as a sort of „Noli me tangere", a precious object which should escape the reckless attack of the anatomical scalpel, and shine entire and intact in the museum, as one of its brightest and most costly ornaments. My Father has indeed subsequently (l. c.) given a number of very important contributions to the morphology of this star-fish; but the materials at his disposal, which only consisted of a fragment of the skeleton of the disc (the bucal ring) of the skeleton of an arm and pieces of a dried arm, were too scanty for any thorough investigation to be made thereon; and his remarks, which are not accompanied by illustrative delineations, are probably not very generally known.

In the summer of 1869 my Father and I together undertook a journey (at public expense) to Hardanger, chiefly in order to procure materials for a renewed study of this singular animal; this object alone being considered worth all the expenses of such a journey. — We succeeded, after repeated dredging in the place indicated, in obtaining several specimens, partly in good preservation, of which one or more should have been submitted to anatomical scrutiny. But unfortunately it did not fall to my Father's lot to execute these in-

* Forhandlinger ved de Skandinaviske Naturforskeres syvende Møde i Christiania 1856 Pag. 209.
[1] Die Klassen und Ordnungen des Thierreichs.
[2] Generelle Morphologie der Organismen.

vestigations, for which he would certainly have been better qualified than any other. A few months later his death, so regrettable for the science, took place, whereby these and many other important examinations which he had just commenced were suddenly interrupted. Already in the preceding year I had, at the fishing place Skraaven in Lofoten, taken up in the dredge, from the considerable depth of 300 fathoms, a quite young specimen of a Brisinga which seemed to exhibit specific differences from the form previously observed, having for instance only 10 arms, and which my Father, in the reasonable belief that the number of arms was in this form as constant as in the B. endecacnemos, denominated preliminarily B. *decacnemos*. It was however not before 1870 that, having found full grown specimens, I succeeded in ascertaining the specific differences of the two forms, and also came to the conviction that the number of the arms in the Lofoten species is, strange to say, and quite contrarily to what has proved to be the case in the form first discovered, subject to very considerable variation; for which reason the specific name appropriated to it by my Father could not be retained. Under the appellation *Brisinga coronata* I noticed it briefly in the year following[1]; reserving to myself to furnish at a subsequent time a more elaborate description accompanied by illustrative delineations. It is this description which I have now the honor to lay before the scientific public. I have not so much had in view to establish by a minute comparative description the independence of the species in relation to that previously described, as by the most thorough and exhaustive investigation possible of the whole organisation of the present species, to furnish a contribution to our general knowledge of the genus Brisinga, in order thereby to gain a more secure stand-point for judging subsequently of the morphology of this remarkable animal form, and of its relation to other Echinoderms.

The tolerably abundant materials which I have had at my disposal, and which in the interest of science I have felt bound to use without any limitation for my anatomical investigations, have enabled me by repeated dissections and preparations, with and without the help of chemical reactives, to ascertain and verify again and again most of the points in the finer anatomic structure

I can here add that the present species has been found also during the expeditions recently organised by the British Government in many places in the great deeps of the Atlantic Ocean, and has been likewise recognised by the chief leader of these expeditions Professor Wyville Thompson, whose thorough acquaintance with the Echinoderms is universally acknowledged, as a species distinct from the form first discovered Brisinga endecacnemos. In a recent very interesting work by the naturalist mentioned, on the results of these expeditions entitled: „The depths of the Sea," Brisinga coronata will be found briefly described under this name proposed by me, with a beautiful woodcut of the animal seen from above.

---

[1] Nye Echinodermer fra den norske Kyst. Chr. Vid. Selsk. Forhandl. f. 1871.

1*

II.

General description of the external form.

(Pysiognomy).

(See Tab. I, fig. 1, Tab. II, fig. 1 & 2).

In its general aspect the present species has on the whole a great resemblance to the *Brisinga endecacnemos* Asbjørnsen as represented in the fauna littoralis Norvegiæ 2ⁿᵈ volume Tab. IX, fig. 1. From a little circular disc of scarcely more than 1 inch diameter, there issue a number of spreading arms or rays (varying from 9 to 12) of an extraordinary length (more than 1 foot) and armed along the edges with several rows of long spines. These arms are very sharply defined, and at the base distinctly instricted; afterwards for a short distance rather strongly enlarged, and then again regularly tapering towards the point; they stand also so close together at the root that there scarcely appears to be any interval between them. On closer examination there will however be observed (see Tab. I, fig. 3) in the angle between 2 arms a small peculiar calcareous plate, which belongs to the skeleton of the disc, and which when the arm is removed (see Tab. I, fig. 6, Tab. III, fig. 1) shews 2 semilunar articulating-surfaces separated by an evident interval. On the upper side this interradial plate rises in a tubercular prominence (Tab. I, fig. 6 d) which is very conspicuous in the upper edge of the disc by its lighter color, and by being for the greater part bare; while the rest of the dorsal surface of the disc is covered with short cylindrical spines growing close together. In one of the corners, at the issue of 2 arms, there appears on the dorsal surface of the disc a rough button-shaped prominence (Tab. I, fig. 3, 4, 6 b) which is the so-called madreporic body. The dorsal side of the arms is very uneven. In their whole length and up to their extreme point (see Tab. I, fig. 12, Tab II, fig. 1 & 2) there are usually found at regular intervals, numerous well defined half cylindrical transverse band-like ridges, which are sometimes variously sinuous, and generally distinguishable by a more intense color than that of the rest of the arm. These transverse ridges appear on closer inspection to be of a soft fleshy consistency; although they also contain calcareous elements in the form of innumerable closely packed microscopic pedicellariæ of the same nature as those which in great numbers cover all the cuticular sheaths of the spines. But besides these soft transverse ridges, there appear in the interior or adoral part of the arms, to about ¼ of their length, a number (10—14) of transverse ribs separated by greater intervals of quite a different nature, namely like strongly projecting solid calcareous beams, which from both sides of the skeleton on the underside of the arms extend at tolerably regular intervals round the dorsal side of the arm, stretching the soft dorsal skin over the interior organs that lie beneath. Along these calcareous transverse ribs (which often (see Tab. II, fig. 4) project very strongly keelshaped on each side, giving to part of the lateral outline of the arms an irregularly sinuous appearance) there is attached a row of more or less elevated spines increasing in length outwards or towards the sides, whereby a certain number of very conspicuous rings of spines are produced over the basal part of the arms, a feature which is very characteristic of the present species, and has also given rise to the specific appellation *coronata*.

If the animal is viewed from the lower side (Tab. I, fig. 2 & 5) there will be seen in the middle a naked membrane (the bucal membrane) circumscribing in the centre a more or less ample circular aperture (f) (the bucal aperture) through which the digestive cavity may be seen. On the sides, this naked and altogether soft part is enclosed in a narrow circular frame of calcareous consistency. This bucal frame, which is formed of the peripheral part of the disc, is not even, but exhibits alternately elevated and depressed surfaces. The former (fig. 5, d. d.) which always lie in the direction of the interval between two arms, are covered with a certain number of rather symmetrically arranged spines of unequal size, which like the spines on the arms, are enveloped in a cuticular sheath thickly covered with pedicellariæ; the innermost of these spines (usually 6 in number) form at the end of the elevated space a fanlike fascicle turned inwards towards the mouth. The depressed spaces of the bucal frame (ibid. c. c.) which are always found just before the insertion of the arms, form the immediate continuation of the wide and deep ambulacral furrows (comp. fig. 2) which run along the whole length of the arms, and at the bottom of the depression there are 2 pairs of tentacles or water-feet extending forwards between the spines on each side. After these 2 pairs of water-feet belonging to the disc, come the water-feet belonging to the arms arranged continuously in the same manner, and at the same distances from each other, and thus forming with those first mentioned 2 uninterrupted rows. On each side of the ambulacral furrow of the arms, and issuing from the thickened border which forms their lateral boundary, being itself formed of the lateral parts of the ambulacral skeleton, are the very strongly developed spines of the arms, in several (usually 4) alternating longitudinal rows (comp. fig. 14). Those in the exterior row are (see fig. 12) fixed just where the dorsal skin of the arm connects itself with the ambulacral skeleton, and in the basal part of the arm always at the extremities of the calcareous transverse ribs: they are the longest of all, and directed outwards to the sides; while those in the other rows decrease rapidly in length, and are directed more downwards. Those in the innermost row (fig. 14. 4) are very small, and directed inwards between the water-feet which issue and extend to some length from the ambulacral furrow. All these spines are, as mentioned, enveloped in a sheath of skin covered with pedicellariae and forming a somewhat enlarged bag beyond their point.

The color of the animal is somewhat variable, but yet so that the dorsal side always exhibits a more or less deep red tint; while the underside of the disc as well as of the arms, is always paler, often quite white. On the dorsal side of the disc the color is usually less pure than on the arms, and frequently goes over to a brownish yellow. In most cases there appears round the periphery of the disc a series of very conspicuous light circular spots corresponding in number with the arms, and shewn by closer examination to be the upper tuberculous projecting part of the above-mentioned interradial calcareous plates situated between each 2 arms, and on which the spines accumulated over all the other parts of the dorsal side of the disc are entirely wanting (see Tab. I. fig. 4. Tab. II, fig. 1 & 2). Only in one place this light spot is absent; as its room is occupied by the strongly prominent madreporic body (b). The color on the dorsal side of the arms goes over in different individuals through several shades from a light red to a deeper coral red, and more rarely to an almost purple tint. The numerous soft transverse ridges have usually, as also the terminal bag of the exterior spines of the arms, a still deeper and often a nearly red violet color; while the calcareous transverse ribs over the basal region are always lighter than the ground color of the arms. The spines are otherwise white; but the water-feet are most frequently of a pale yellowish color.

Such is briefly the exterior appearance of this magnificent animal. It is however seldom that we can see it as now viewed entire and uninjured, with all the arms in their natural connexion with the disc. Not a single one of the specimens collected by me have I been able to preserve entire, although every possible precaution has been employed; but in all, the arms have been more or less completely separated from the disc, as was also the case with the specimens hitherto preserved of the other species B. endecacnemos. In this condition the animal appears like a confused heap of detached parts entangled together, giving only a very imperfect idea of the splendid exterior of this star-fish; and even the specimens artificially recomposed of the B. endecacnemos in the Bergen Museum, bear so evidently the stamp of manufacture, that they can not give us a completely correct representation of the true original appearance of the animal. I have however sometimes had opportunity to admire this remarkable Asteride in its full beauty at the moment when it was taken up from the depths of the ocean. In a few cases I have been so fortunate, when the dredge at length came up to the gunnel of the boat from the enormous depth of 300 fathoms, as to see it lying in the dredge-net, whole and uninjured as it had been crawling about on the bottom, with all its parts in their natural connexion. But the animal is then, as will easily be understood (after being drawn up from total darkness and from the tranquil depth of the ocean to the clear light of day and to the disturbed surface of the water) put into so unnatural a state for all its functions of life, that even the slightest mechanical incitements will have a disturbing influence on its essentially loosely connected organism. However carefully therefore I have acted in endeavoring to lift up this gem of the ocean, I have never succeeded in obtaining it entire. On the slightest touch, all the arms usually break off at their junction with the disc; so that the latter is most frequently quite detached from them. Only in a very few instances, by employing the utmost care, and by placing the specimen immediately in spirit, I have been able to obtain one or more arms in natural connexion with the disc. I have thus, as a great rarity, got one single young specimen preserved, with 4 arms attached to the disc. This is the specimen from which the 3 first figures in Tab. I have been delineated.

III

Special description of the organs.
(Organology).

I. The Skeleton System.
(Tab. IV. fig. 1—22 and Tab. VI).

The solid support for the disc, as well as for the arms, is composed of numerous calcareous pieces more or less firmly connected with each other, and forming together the so-called ambulacral skeleton. On the disc this skeleton forms a narrow exterior frame or ring (fig. 1, 2 & 3) consisting of calcareous pieces immovably connected: and to the outer side or periphery of this ring the ambulacral skeleton of the arms is attached. The latter skeleton (see fig. 15—22), which occupies the lower side of the arms from the base to the extreme point, consists of numerous sections or joints connected, to a certain extent movably, with each other by elastic bands, and forming the so-called ambulacral vertebræ, of which each is again composed of a certain number of symmetrically arranged calcareous pieces. Both the ambulacral skeleton of the arms and that of the disc are externally covered with a smooth tendinous skin, like a thin envelope, firmly attached by growth, or as it were a kind of periosteum, which can only be entirely removed by long maceration or by employing chemical reactives. We shall now regard the ambulacral skeleton of the arms, and that of the disc each for itself.

a. The ambulacral Skeleton of the arms.
(Tab. IV. fig. 15—22).

As already noticed, the ambulacral skeleton of the arms consists, like that of the other star-fishes, of a series of similar successive sections or joints which have been called vertebræ by reason of a certain general resemblance which the skeleton of the arm exhibits to the vertebral column of a vertebrated animal; a resemblance which is certainly more remarkable in the present Asteride than in any other (comp. fig. 15, 16 & 17). These vertebræ together form the boundary of the wide and deep ambulacral furrow which runs along the ventral side of the arms, and in the bottom of which appear the holes or ambulacral pores situated in pairs and indicating the attachment of the water-feet (see fig. 16). Each vertebra (Tab. V, fig. 3—6) is composed of 2 ambulacral plates (aa) firmly connected with each other by a suture in the middle, forming the upper convexity of the ventral furrow, and of 2 thick cylindrical adambulacral plates (ad ad) which form the borders of the furrow on each side. In addition to these there are on the 2 interior vertebræ of the arms (fig. 15—17) a pair of peculiar plates (c c) situated on each side above the adambulacral plates, and which, according to their place, must be considered as answering to the dorsal marginal plates in other star-fishes. The connexion between the individual vertebræ is effected by means of smooth articulating surfaces which in the circumference are partially attached to each other by elastic muscular bands. Of these joint-surfaces there may be distinguished (see fig. 19—20) at each end of the vertebra, 4: namely 2 central, situated close together (a a) whereby the 2 dorsal parts of the ambulacral plates which meet in the middle are connected with those of the preceding and of the following vertebra, and 2 lateral (b b) whereby the adambulacral plates of 2 vertebræ are connected with each other. This last connexion seems to be the most movable, and is effected with considerably inclined joint-surfaces. On the adoral side of the interior vertebra of the arm, there is moreover a 3ᵈ pair of articulating surfaces (c c) connecting the dorsal marginal plates with the skeleton of the disc.

If we regard the skeleton of the arm in its entirety, it exhibits on the upper part (see fig. 15) along the middle, a rather high ridge or keel with a deep medial furrow. This ridge represents the central part of the vertebræ of the arm, and is formed by the dorsal part of the 2 contiguous ambulacral plates. On each side of this ridge the skeleton of the arm is perforated by a series of circular apertures, which on the ventral side (see fig. 16) appear at the bottom of the ambulacral furrow as the ambulacral pores, situated close together in pairs, for the water-feet. These apertures are separated from each other by narrow partitions inclining downwards and outwards from the dorsal ridge, with their flat enlarged extremities resting on, and attached to the thickened margin, formed by the adambulacral plates, which makes the lateral boundary of the ambulacral furrow. At the bottom of this furrow there is along the middle a narrow and rather deep furrow or semi-canal, which in some places is covered with connecting ligaments. It is destined to contain the radial ambulacral vessel which extends through the whole length of the arm, and from which the water-feet with their ampollæ are supplied with water.

The limits of the individual vertebræ are, both on the dorsal and on the ventral side, very distinct, and even externally indicated by evident intervals or slits covered with elastic fibres, which allow the whole arm to be bent or extended. On the dorsal ridge these slits have (see fig. 15) an inward and somewhat converging direction, and are especially very

2

conspicuous at the edges. By these slits the whole dorsal ridge is divided into a series of successive sections, which are cylindrical or somewhat enlarged at both extremities, and have the appearance of corpora in the spine of a vertebrated animal. From the middle of each of these sections there issues on each side — wonderfully like the transverse processes on a vertebra — one of the above mentioned partitions which separate the ambulacral pores from each other. The flattened enlarged extremity of these partitions, which thus represent the lateral parts of the ambulacral plates, rests on the thickened lateral margin of the skeleton of the arm always at the junction of the adambulacral plates of 2 vertebræ; so that only a single adambulacral plate lies between them. The above-mentioned ambulacral pores will thus be bounded outwardly only by one single adambulacral plate, and otherwise by the ambulacral plates of 2 successive vertebræ. As regards the form of the adambulacral plates, it is on the whole cylindrical: but the interior surface, which makes the lateral boundary of the apertures for the suction feet, is rather strongly concaved. They are separated from each other by distinct inclined slits, which are covered with elastic fibres, and which are, especially at the extremity of the skeleton of the arm, very wide.

As already noticed, the 2 interior vertebræ of the arm are distinguished by a somewhat shorter and broader form of the dorsal part of the ambulacral plates, and by each of them having, immediately above the adambulacral plates, a distinctly developed dorsal marginal plate (see fig. 17). On the interior vertebra of the arm this dorsal marginal plate (c¹) is largest, of trapezoidal form, tapering outwards and having a rather large semilunar articulating surface, whereby it is articulated with a corresponding marginal plate on the outer side of the disc; at the aboral extremity it is firmly connected (often quite grown together) with the next marginal plate (c²) which is considerably narrower, and of an obtusely conical form. These 2 pairs of marginal plates, which are also very distinctly apparent on the exterior of the arm (see Tab. 1. fig. 12 b, Tab. 2, fig. 1 & 2) are certainly intended to effect a firmer connexion between the disc and the enormously developed arms, than would otherwise be possible, if the connexion only existed between the ambulacral and the adambulacral plates.

The skeleton of the arm has moreover in its whole length a tolerably uniform appearance, excepting only that it tapers gradually towards the extremity, whereby also the individual vertebræ are successively reduced in size. The extreme point of the skeleton of the arm exhibits however, when more closely examined, a very abnormal constitution (fig. 21 & 22); the single vertebræ being here fused together in a rather large convex plate, which serves as a protection for a peculiar organ of sense afterwards described.

b. The ambulacral skeleton of the disc.
(The bucal ring).
(Tab. IV, fig. 1—14).

When the skin and the interior soft parts are removed from the disc, there remains a rather narrow circular frame or ring (fig. 1—3), of a firm calcareous consistency, representing the ambulacral skeleton of the disc. This frame has (see fig. 2) its lower side flattened horisontally, and divided into regularly alternating elevated and depressed spaces, of which the former (a) taper a little inwards; while the latter (b) are of more uniform breadth. At the bottom of each of the depressed spaces there appear 4 circular apertures, situated in pairs and indicating the attachment of the water-feet of the disc (see also fig. 5). The upper side of the bucal ring is not horisontal, but rising somewhat obliquely inwards. From the most salient interior part of the bucal ring, the interior wall is inclined obliquely downwards; while the much lower exterior wall is more perpendicular. A section of the ring will thus represent a quadrangle with 2 longer and 2 shorter sides. The 2 longer sides represent the lower and interior, and the 2 shorter sides, the upper and exterior sides (comp. fig. 10 & 11). The interior wall of the bucal ring is (see fig. 1, 7 & 8) rather even and smooth, but has nearer to the lower side a horizontal deep groove or semi-canal (x) extending in a circle round the whole ring, and having at the lower edge a thickened, and inwardly somewhat salient border (y) which serves as attachment for the thin strongly contractile bucal skin. This groove is destined to receive the circular ambulacral vessel situated inside of the disc, and which, by means of the stone-canal, stands in connexion with the madreporic body on the dorsal side of the disc. At the bottom of the groove there appears, opposite to the middle of each of the depressed spaces on the under-side of the bucal ring, a small circular aperture (fig. 8. o.) indicating the place whence the ambulacral vessels radiating to the arms issue from the annular vessel.

The exterior, (as partly also the upper) side of the bucal ring is very uneven, with numerous elevations and depressions, which however soon appear to have a very regular arrangement. If lines are drawn along the middle of the alternately depressed and elevated spaces on the lower side, and continued round the whole ring, it will be found that these unevennesses correspond exactly to each other on each side of the lines. If the lines are continued outwards (the arms being considered as in connexion with the disc) then the lines which bisect the depressed ventral spaces will also bisect the ambulacral skeleton of the arms; while the lines which bisect the elevated ventral spaces will be continued out through the intervals between the arms (see Tab. V, fig. 1—2). We may therefore, for the sake of facility, preliminarily call the former the radial spaces of the disc, and the latter the interradial spaces. On closer inspection of the skeleton of the disc, it will be perceived that the guiding lines

2*

above referred to are by no means imaginary, but really exist in the form of evident sutures. On the radial spaces these medial sutures may be traced round the whole ring; but in the interradial spaces these sutures are interrupted on the upper side by a narrow single piece, which we will call the wedge-plate (fig. 4, 6, 7, 8, 9 k) just forming the angle at the issue of 2 arms, and the upper tubercular salient extremity of which is always, as before remarked, very distinctly apparent on the exterior of the disc. Besides the sutures mentioned, which thus bisect the radial and interradial spaces of the disc, there may still be observed on closer examination a number of other sutures indicating that the bucal ring is composed of a great number of single pieces. Of these sutures there are some which go more or less across the ring: others, which have quite a different direction, running along the upper or lower side of the ring or parallel with its exterior or interior edge. The last sutures, which are the most distinctly marked of them all, will be found to lie all in about the same plane, and are especially very conspicuous on the upper side of the radial spaces, and on the lower side of the interradial spaces. The result is that each of these spaces is also transversely divided into 2, or consists of 2 successive sections. If we only consider the sutures running along the ring, we shall thus find that the latter is composed of 2 concentric rings firmly attached to each other: the inner being both higher and wider than the outer.

If such a bucal ring, with a part of the outer tendinous skin still adhering to it, be placed in a concentrated solution of potass, the single pieces connected by suture will after a short time separate completely from each other, and instead of a continuous ring there will appear only a confused heap of numerous single calcareous pieces of various size and form. The bucal ring is thus resolved into its simple elements, the appreciation of which will now present considerable difficulties.

But if the operation be suspended a little before, it may happen that larger or smaller parts of the bucal ring can be obtained with the single pieces in natural connexion with each other, and yet connected so loosely that one piece after the other may be separated from the rest with the greatest ease.

On examining and comparing a number of such parts, it will soon be found easy to get some idea of the apparently extremely complicated structure of the bucal ring, especially on comparing therewith one of the so-called ambulacral vertebræ of the skeleton of the arm.

If we consider the bucal ring in its natural connexion with the ambulacral skeleton of the arms (see Tab. V, fig. 1—2), we shall easily be able to ascertain that it is chiefly composed of double sets of similar vertebræ to those which form the skeleton of the arms; so that each arm tinued inwards by two ambulacral vertebræ entering into the formation of the bucal ring is con- and therefore immovably connected with each other and with their neighbors. The exterior set of these vertebræ of the disc correspond really in almost every respect with the interior free vertebræ of the arm, and can therefore, morphologically speaking, be more properly said to belong to the arms than to the disc: which is also, as will subsequently be shewn, confirmed by the development. On the other hand, the interior set of the vertebræ exhibit several peculiarities in their form, as also the insertion of single calcareous plates between them, to which nothing analogous is to be observed in the other vertebræ, and which are destined to attach them still more firmly together.

If we once more view the bucal ring from the lower side (fig. 2 & 5) it will be easily perceived that the radial or depressed spaces make the interior continuation of the ambulacral furrows of the arms, and consequently are formed in the middle by the ambulacral plates of the two vertebræ mentioned; while the elevated or interradial spaces are formed by the contact of the adambulacral plates of 2 pairs of adjacent vertebræ. If we then turn the bucal ring, and view it from above (fig. 1 & 4) we shall observe, on that part of it which lies just over the ventral furrow, the dorsal convex part of the ambulacral plates (a a) of the 2 vertebræ in contact, continuing the dorsal ridge of the skeleton of the arms inwards. On each side of this raised part there are (at the extreme outside) 2 deep cavities which when closely examined are found to extend through the whole thickness of the bucal ring, and appear on the lower side as the before-mentioned holes, situated in pairs in the ventral furrow, for the insertion of the water-feet. In this manner the double series of holes or ambulacral pores that perforate the skeleton of the arm in its whole length, is thus likewise continued inwards on the bucal ring. Inside of these holes, the ambulacral plates (a¹) of the interior vertebræ come on each side in contact with a peculiar plate (m) to which there is nothing corresponding in the other vertebræ, and which we may call the parietal-plate; as it contributes in an essential degree to form the interior wall of the bucal ring. It comes here in contact (see fig. 7) with the corresponding plate on the adjacent vertebræ, while these 2 parietal-plates are separated above by a 3ʳᵈ equally peculiar single plate (k) wedged in between them, which plate we have previously denominated the wedge-plate. With the exterior end of this plate (which lies just in the angle between 2 arms) there are again connected 2 small plates (r) belonging to 2 adjacent vertebræ of the exterior set, each articulated with one of the interior dorsal marginal plates situated on 2 adjacent arms; for which reason we may also regard those small plates observed on the exterior side of the bucal ring as corresponding to the dorsal marginal plates on the disc of other starfishes.

The bucal ring is thus in a 10-armed specimen composed of 20 complete ambulacral vertebræ; 30 peculiar plates inserted between the interior vertebræ, and 20 dorsal marginal plates. The individual plates of which the bucal ring is composed, are therefore as follow:

Plates.			Interior vertebræ.	Exterior vertebræ.
Ambulacral plates	. . .	. .	20	20
Adambulacral plates		. .	20	20
Parietal plates	.	. .	20	-
Wedge plates	. . .	. . .	10	-
Dorsal marginal plates	.	.	-	20
			70 + 60	

Together 130 single plates.

The more particular relation of the 2 sets of vertebræ which enter into the composition of the bucal ring, and of the single calcareous plates belonging to and connecting them, is as follows.

The exterior vertebræ which, as already noticed, should properly be considered as belonging to the arms (although they always remain fixed to the skeleton of the disc when the arms are detached) are considerably shorter and lower than the interior vertebræ (comp. fig. 10). In their structure they correspond very closely with the interior vertebræ of the arms, with which they are to a certain degree movably connected in nearly their whole height. The articulating surfaces which appear distinctly in every detached disc on the exterior side (see Tab. I, fig. 6, Tab. III, fig. 1) exhibit therefore also in their form and arrangement the most exact conformity with those on the adoral side of the interior vertebræ of the arms (Tab. IV, fig. 20). It is easy to distinguish (see also Tab. IV, fig. 6) the strongly convex central part (a²), formed by the 2 ambulacral plates uniting in the middle, with its 2 large vertical articulating surfaces. The side parts inclining outwards and downwards from this central part, form also here the boundaries between 2 pairs of ambulacral pores, of which the interior pair belongs to the disc; while the exterior pair is destined for the attachment of the 1st pair of water-feet of the arm. At the end of these side parts lie the strongly developed adambulacral plates (ad²) which exhibit a large, somewhat inclined, roundly triangular smooth articulating surface, whereby these plates are articulated with the adambulacral plates of the 1st vertebra of the arm. They are considerably wider than the latter, and are in immediate contact with the nearest adambulacral plates of the 2 adjacent vertebræ, with which they are firmly connected by suture. Above the adambulacral plates there are lastly the before-mentioned dorsal marginal plates (r) situated one on each side furthest outwards, and exhibiting a small semilunar articulatory surface, whereby these plates are articulated with the corresponding plates on the 1st joint of the arm. These plates also are, at their interior extremity, in immediate contact with the nearest dorsal marginal plates of the adjacent vertebræ and immovably connected with the same, as also with the extremity of the wedge-plate (k) belonging to the interior vertebræ.

In the interior set of vertebræ, which are properly those that belong specially to the disc, we can likewise distinguish (see fig. 9) a pair of ambulacral plates (a¹) and a pair of adambulacral plates (ad¹); while there are no proper dorsal marginal plates. In place of the latter, there are between each vertebra and its neighbor inserted 3 peculiar plates which we have denominated the parietal plates (m) and the wedge-plate (k). ·

The ambulacral plates are not only considerably longer (see fig. 10) but also higher and broader than on the exterior vertebræ; while the adambulacral plates (see fig. 5 ad¹) are much narrower, and terminate in a somewhat unevenly truncated edge, which projects freely under the thickened margin (y) and to which are attached the spines radiating towards the mouth (the bucal spines) (see fig. 2). Each of the ambulacral plates is, as before-mentioned, connected at one extremity by distinct suture with a so-called parietal plate. This is (see fig. 4, 6, 7, 8 m) quite narrow above, and here contributes to form the boundary of the interior pair of ambulacral pores, but is considerably enlarged on the interior side of the bucal ring; so that these plates contribute essentially at this part to form its interior wall, (see fig. 7), as also the above mentioned inwardly salient margin (y), which makes the lower boundary of the circular semi-canal for the ambulacral vessel of the disc, appears to be formed exclusively by these plates. On the other hand the ambulacral plates themselves (a¹) taper here rapidly, as the sutures between them and the parietal plates converge downwards towards the holes, situated in the semi-canal mentioned, for the radial ambulacral vessels (o). Each parietal plate comes close up on the interior wall of the bucal ring to the adjoining one on the adjacent vertebra, yet without being immediately connected with the same; as there is always between them a very narrow crevice leading into a rather spacious cavity in the interior of the bucal ring (see fig. 11, l). These parietal plates are however above separated from each other by the insertion between them of a single peculiar plate (k), which may in a manner be said to continue or terminate the series of dorsal marginal plates inwardly. This plate, which we have called the wedge-plate, is (see fig. 12, 13, 14) quite narrow, in the middle somewhat constricted and nearly cylindrical; while the upper part is enlarged to a tubercular prominence with corners drawn out on each side. Its exterior surface is smooth and convex, while its interior surface is somewhat uneven, and slopes from each side upwards towards the middle (see fig. 13). It is wedged in with its upper part between 2 parietal plates, so as to extend round the dorsal edge of the bucal ring, and a little way down on the inner surface (see fig. 7, 8); its lower extremity is truncated, and on each side connected by sutures with the lower lateral extremity of an ambulacral plate of the interior set of vertebræ; while it connects itself in the middle with 2 of the dorsal marginal plates belonging to the exterior set of vertebræ.

2. The cuticular system.

The cuticular system or Perisoma of the Brisinga is composed, as in other star-fishes of the proper integument or skin, and of various calcareous parts which are partly imbedded in the interior of the skin, partly raised above the same in form of spines ridges or microscopic pincers, and which exhibit both in structure and function very marked differences. The integument itself also shows a rather different structure in different regions of the body, and we may thus properly distinguish two principal sorts of integuments, the dorsal and the ventral.

a. The dorsal integument.

The skin which forms the upper covering of the disc and arms, is of very considerable firmness, almost leather-like, and shews itself (see Tab. 1, fig. 8) to be composed of 2 distinct layers or strata, a thicker and firmer interior layer, and a thinner and less substantial exterior layer: the former of fibrous, and the latter of cellular structure. In both these strata of the skin there are imbedded various calcareous parts, which will be more particularly noticed hereafter. In the middle of the disc and of the arms this dorsal skin is extended quite freely over the subjacent internal organs, and thus forms the immediate boundary of the perivisceral cavity in this part; while it joins the ambulacral skeleton on the sides, growing together with the tendinous membrane that envelopes the skeleton like a periosteum.

The internal stratum of the skin is evidently composed of a contractile tissue; white shining fibres of great tenacity and elasticity being interwoven with each other in different directions; it is especially in the dorsal skin of the disc very strongly developed. No distinct pores could be detected in the same, either on the disc or on the arms.

The external stratum or epidermis is of a much softer and more fragile consistency and partly lined with fine vibratile cilia. It covers as a continuous layer all the unevennesses of the body; and all the spines which issue from the surface of the body thereby receive their peculiar sheath-like envelope. On the dorsal side of the arms it forms moreover the peculiar transversal semi-cylindrical fleshy ridges, especially characteristic of this species, which are traceable even to the extreme point of the arm.

b. The ventral integument.

From the integuments properly so-called we distinguish the cuticular stratum, which is found on the ventral side inside the ambulacral skeleton, partly lining the bottom of the ambulacral furrows and partly surrounding the oral aperture as the so-called bucal membrane. This ventral cuticle is of much finer and thinner consistency and without any trace of calcareous deposits. In the ambulacral furrows it appears as a thin transparent membrane without any distinct structure; while the bucal membrane is remarkable for a high degree of contractility, for which reason also it is interwoven with numerous fine concentric and radial muscular fibres; it will be more particularly described hereafter.

c. The calcareous parts belonging to the integument.

Of the various calcareous deposits in question we may distinguish 3 principal groups; 1) the calcareous deposits in the interior stratum of the skin. 2) the spines issuing from the surface of the body and 3) the peculiar microscopic organs found in the exterior stratum of the skin, which we call pedicellariæ.

α. The interior calcareous elements of the skin.

The formations classed in this category, which correspond to the more or less developed calcareous net in other star-fishes, consist of variously formed calcareous deposits in the interior stratum of the skin, serving partly for the insertion of the dorsal spines, and partly as a frame-work to extend the skin over the subjacent interior organs.

In the dorsal skin of the disc, we find these calcareous parts (see Tab. I, fig. 8, 9 a) in the shape of small truncated cones, situated close together and traversing the interior stratum of skin in its whole thickness, yet without being connected wich each other or forming any proper calcareous net. Each of these calcareous parts consists apparently of numerous small cemented calcareous granules (see fig. 9 a): and on the narrower upper extremity, there is always articulated one of the small dorsal spines which project beyond the skin of the disc. By means of these close-lying calcareous parts, the dorsal skin of the disc acquires a very considerable degree of solidity; although it retains its elasticity and flexibility owing to their not being connected with each other.

The calcareous deposits found in the dorsal skin of the arms present quite a different appearance. These calcareous parts are however essentially confined to the basal part of the arms: while the rest of the dorsal skin of the arms is quite soft and flexible, and lies close to the subjacent ambulacral skeleton. But in the basal part of the arm, which contains a number of important and some very strongly developed internal organs, (the radial cæca and the organs of generation) it was necessary for the skin to have an internal support, in order the better to protect these organs, and to preserve them from outward pressure. Therefore the calcareous elements deposited in the skin appear in these parts in a very peculiar form especially adapted for such purpose, namely as continuous solid arched transverse beams connected on each side with the ambulacral skeleton, and, being placed

3

at a suitable distance from each other, extend the whole skin like a sheltering roof above the said internal organs.

These very strong calcareous transverse beams, which undoubtedly, in spite of their very different appearance, are to be referred to the same category as the isolated calcareous particles in the dorsal skin of the disc (both formations corresponding to the calcareous net of the normal star-fish) are also (see Tab. I, fig. 12. Tab. II, fig. 1, 2 & 4) very conspicuous on the exterior as more or less strongly projecting transverse ribs. Like the calcareous particles in the skin of the disc, these transverse ribs give also issue to spines, which are always arranged in a single transverse row along the rib. With respect to the extent, number and form of these transverse ribs, there is considerable variation. Usually they are distinct on all the basal fourth part of the arm, and from 10 to 14 in number. They are always placed at some distance from each other; so that generally there are 2 vertebræ between each of them and its neighbor. As to their form, they are often more or less sinuous, more rarely forked on one of the sides. Sometimes they are incomplete or interrupted at parts; and this seems to be the rule with those furthest from the disc; the sides only being developed, and one of the above-named soft transverse ridges forming the continuation in the middle. They are, as noticed, firmly attached on each side by a ligament to the ambulacral skeleton; and their somewhat enlarged extremity gives at this point of connexion issue to an unusually long spine directed outwards and sidewise, which we will call the marginal spine, as it proceeds from the margin of the arm. These marginal spines are however, as will be seen, not confined to the basal part of the arm, but are continued also along the edges of the whole remaining part of the arm, even to its extreme point; and on closer examination we shall find that they are also here not attached to the ambulacral skeleton itself, but to small calcareous pieces, connected with it at regular intervals, which may therefore be considered as a sort of rudiments of the so strongly developed calcareous ribs on the basal part.

5. The spines.

The various spines projecting over the surface of the body, issue partly from the calcareous particles deposited in the interior stratum of the skin, partly direct from the ambulacral skeleton itself; and they are always more or less movably connected with the same. Their form and length vary in the different parts of the body; but the proper calcareous spine is always enveloped as in a sheath by the exterior stratum of skin, which usually forms a bag projecting far beyond the point of the spine, and, like the rest of the cuticular sheath, covered with numerous pedicellariæ.

All the spines articulated with the ambulacral skeleton, issue from the ventral side, and are here attached to the adambulacral plates which form the lateral boundaries of the ventral furrows, for which reason also the corresponding spines in other Asteridæ are usually called furrow-papillæ or furrow-spines. They are situated in the Brisinga alternately, forming along the arms on each side of the ventral furrow 3 rather regular longitudinal rows (see Tab, I, fig. 14). There will most frequently be found on each adambulacral plate 3 such spines (ibid. 2, 3, 4) situated in an oblique transverse row, and diminishing rapidly in size towards the medial line. Each of these spines belongs thus naturally to a different longitudinal row. The exterior and largest of them (2) issues from about the middle of the ventral side of the adambulacral plate, and is here articulated with a very distinct projecting rounded knob or tubercle: it is usually directed obliquely downwards and a little outwards, and in the exterior part of the arm exceeds the breadth of the arm. The next spine (3) is considerably smaller, scarcely $\frac{1}{2}$ as long, and usually pointing straight downward. And lastly the interior spine (4) issuing from the interior adoral angle of the adambulacral plate, is very small, and points inwards towards the ventral furrow between the extended water-feet. In very young specimens (see fig. 2) these 2 innermost spines are yet undeveloped: so that there is only a single longitudinal row of furrow-spines along the middle of the adambulacral areas. But in older specimens, the number of the furrow-spines often increases considerably: so that along the interior edge of the adambulacral plates there may be found 2, 3 or even 4 small spines, all apparently belonging to the interior longitudinal row (see Tab. IV, fig. 16).

On the lower side of the disc (see Tab. I. fig. 2 & 5) these furrow-spines are continued on each side of the ambulacral furrows up to their extremities at the bucal area. They are also here attached to the 2 pairs of adambulacral plates which form the boundary of the ventral furrow of the disc; so that a somewhat larger spine always issues from the middle of each of these plates; while the others stand nearer to the edge, which is turned towards the ventral furrow (see Tab. IV. fig. 2). The number of these spines is also here somewhat variable according to age. But from the interior border (turned towards the mouth) of the innermost adambulacral plate, there always issue a certain number (usually 3) larger spines pointing horisontally inwards towards the mouth, and which together with the corresponding spines on the adjacent adambulacral plate, form at the end of each of the interradial spaces a regular fan-like outspread fascicle of usually 6 spines, corresponding to the bucal spines in other star-fish.

All the spines mentioned are in their structure completely similar. The calcareous spine itself is (see Tab. I, fig. 15—21) slender, shaped like an awl or like a needle; not echinulated, but smooth and shining and moreover distinctly striped longitudinally. These stripes, which often go somewhat obliquely, or rather spirally, are raised smooth ribs; and in the intervals between them, there may be observed, when strongly magnified, rows of transversely oval holes traversing the hyaline calcareous net of which the spine is composed. Only at the extreme point there appear when strongly magnified (see fig. 17) some short irregularly placed points; otherwise the spine is quite smooth. At the base the spine is somewhat enlarged, and has a depressed articulating surface, whereby it is articulated with a corresponding elevated knob or tubercle on the ambulacral skeleton. The articulating surfaces are in the periphery connected by tendinous muscular ligaments, whereby the spines can be moved in various directions. The thick sheath formed by the exterior stratum of the skin (cuticle) which envelopes the spine, terminates always in a somewhat enlarged bag, often prolonged far beyond the extremity of the spine, and not unfrequently curved in various ways, sometimes nearly at right angles (fig. 18).

The very long spines, attached along the sides of the arms, which with reference to their position we have called marginal spines, are also of exactly the same structure. These spines are however, as already noticed, not attached to the ambulacral skeleton, like the furrow spines, but, in the basal part of the arm. to the extremities of the calcareous transverse ribs, and further out, to peculiar small calcareous plates connected by ligaments with the adambulacral plates. They form (see Tab. II. fig. 1 & 2) on each side a single row from the base of the arms to their extreme point.

If we consider these marginal spines together with the furrow-spines, the arms (see Tab. I. fig. 14) will appear furnished on each side with 4 rows of spines, of which those in the exterior row (the marginal spines) (1) are the longest. As the marginal spines do not, like the furrow-spines, correspond in number with the adambulacral plates, but most frequently are to the latter only in proportion of 1 to 3, their number is also always smaller than that of the furrow-spines belonging to a single row. At the base of the arms they are only slightly developed, but increase rapidly in length outwards until towards the middle of the length of the arm, where they are 3—4 times as long as the arm is broad. Further outwards they then gradually decrease in length, until they become rudimentary again towards the point (see Tab. II. fig. 6).

The dorsal spines of the arms, are, as noticed, only attached along the calcareous transverse ribs, and thus confined to the basal part alone.

They form here always only single rows, and usually increase in length outwards, but without attaining to nearly the length of the marginal spines and of the exterior furrow-spines. They seem to be of somewhat stouter structure than the other spines of the arms, with a less developed cuticular sheath and fewer pedicellariæ.

The spines attached to the dorsal skin of the disc are however rather different. These are quite short, situated vertically, all about of the same length and close together, whereby the whole of the dorsal side acquires, as it were, a hairy appearance, see Tab. I. fig. 4. 6). They are of cylindrical form with a bluntly rounded extremity. This form is however chiefly attributable to the thick cuticular sheath in which they are enveloped. On applying a solution of potass, which renders the exterior cuticle transparent, the interior proper calcareous spine (see fig. 8, 9 b) will appear attached by a somewhat enlarged base to one of the calcareous pieces (fig. 9 a) imbedded in the interior stratum of the skin. It is finely reticulated, narrowest in the middle, while the extremity is somewhat enlarged, terminating in a greater or less number of fine points (fig. 9, 10, 11).

7. The Pedicellariæ.

These organs, which are very characteristic of the proper star-fishes, and which are entirely wanting in the brittle stars or Ophiuræ, appear in the Brisinga in the greatest abundance, as well on the disc as on the arms. They are observed in quite enormous masses in the cuticular sheath of all the furrow-spines and marginal spines, giving to it, as it were, a granulated appearance; likewise in extraordinary abundance on the soft cuticular ridges which surround the dorsal side of the arms in their whole length; they are observed in much smaller numbers also, distributed over the remaining part of the skin, and on and between the dorsal spines of the disc. (see Tab. 1, fig. 8 a).

They are in the present species of Brisinga extremely small, scarcely more than $\frac{1}{10}$'" long, and exhibit a remarkably complicated structure. Of all the known forms of pedicellariæ they seem in their structure to resemble most those described by my Father in the genus Pedicellaster; and, like them, belong to the principal form designated by Joh. Müller with the denomination Pedicellariæ forcipatæ, characterised by 2 pincer-like branches provided with teeth that fit to each other and enabled by means of a peculiar muscular apparatus to move towards each other, and thereby to grasp and to hold small objects.

On each pedicellaria there may be distinguished (see Tab. IV, fig. 23 & 24) a thicker exterior part or capitulum, and a much thinner flexible stem, whereby the pedicellaria is attached to the skin. The exterior enlarged part which represents the proper body of the pedicellaria, exhibits usually an oval form with the greatest thickness at the base, and the extremity laterally somewhat compressed. On closer examination this part appears to consist of 2 broad more or less gaping lobes, each of which envelopes the extremity of one of the jaws of the forceps; the dentated edges here advancing freely from the fleshy envelope, so as to work directly against each other. If a dilated solution of potass be applied to such an isolated pedicellaria, whereby the exterior cuticular sheath will be rendered transparent, the calcareous pieces which form the foundation of the pedicellaria will be seen very distinctly inside the sheath in the upper enlarged part or capitulum; these calcareous pieces (see fig. 25—29) are always 3 in number, namely 2 uniform side-pieces (a) which represent the 2 movable jaws, and a 3^d unpaired calcareous piece (c), which is inserted between them and serves both as articulation for the side pieces and attachment for the muscles (m) that move them. All 3 calcareous pieces are hyaline and more or less perforated with small circular or oval apertures. The side pieces (a) are thickest in the middle, and have in that part on the inside a vertical dentated edge, which, when the jaws of the forceps are bent towards each other, meets the corresponding edge on the other side-piece. On the pedicellariæ of the arms (fig. 27—29) this edge is quite short and evenly rounded, while on the pedicellariæ of the disc (fig. 25, 26) it is considerably longer, quite straight, and projecting at the anterior extremity in a short lobe. Immediately below this dentated edge, the side piece is attached to the middle piece (c) so as to form with it a sort of hinge, which allows of a very considerable mobility in a fixed direction. The side-pieces are continued forward into the forceps, which exhibits a strong curvature inwards and has a kind of short cylindrical neck, after which it is enlarged at the extremity almost in the form of a gouge. Along the upper nearly straight truncated and sharp edge and a little way down on each side, the extremity of the jaw of the forceps is armed with a row of pointed teeth bent inwards, of which that situated at each corner is largest, (see fig 30). When both jaws are curved towards each other, (see fig 25. 27) these teeth fit accurately between each other, and can thereby hold the smallest objects fast. In like manner the above-mentioned vertical dentated edges proceeding from the middle, meet in the middle line, while there always remains between these and the extremity of the forceps a considerable open space. Herein the pedicellariæ in the Brisinga differ essentially from those of the genus Pedicellaster and Asterias, where the forceps closes in its whole length. From each side-piece there issues downwards a large plate-shaped process (b) directed obliquely inwards, yet not lying in the same axis as the proper forceps, but forming with it an obtuse angle (see fig. 26). At the base this process is somewhat instricted, and distinctly marked out from the rest of the side-piece by a small sinus in the exterior edge, in which one extremity of the middle piece (c) fits. Inside of the exterior convex border there are a certain number of larger and smaller oval apertures which have a somewhat constant arrangement on all the pedicellariæ. At the enlarged plate-like extremity of this process there is attached an evident muscle (fig. 26 m) the other end of which is inserted in the opposite similarly plate-formed part of the middle piece (c). By the contraction of this muscle the jaws of the forceps are moved inwards and towards each other, turning round the extremities of the middle piece as on a hinge. When the muscle is relaxed, the jaws separate again from each other, whereby the side-pieces are brought nearly into a horisontal position (see fig. 28). The middle piece (c) inserted between the two side-pieces and serving as an articulation for them, is much smaller: it is situated transversally, and exhibits on the under-side 2 plate-shaped enlargements separated by a deep sinus in the middle, and like the lower process of the side-pieces, perforated with small apertures, which are usually arranged in a double row along the lower curved edge. These plate-like enlargements, which serve for the insertion of the muscles that move the jaws of the forceps, do not however lie exactly in the same plane, but have in relation to the axis of the middle-piece a somewhat oblique position. Viewed from above (fig. 29) this piece exhibits therefore a narrow nearly cross-like shape with its greatest width in the middle, and the rapidly tapering ends, curved each to its side, partially embracing the side-pieces in the middle. From the upper side there issue 2 short obtuse processes directed obliquely outwards and leaning on each side against the inner vertical dentated edge: they partially cover each other, when the middle piece is viewed from the broad side, and together appear like an elevation in the middle of the upper edge. (see fig. 25. 27).

3. The water system.

The water system in the Brisinga exhibits in the main the same normal features as that of the proper star-fish. We have here to distinguish 1) the ambulacral vessels, and the exterior parts which stand in connexion with the same; 2) the water-feet with their ampollæ, and 3) the madreporic body with the stone-canal.

a. The ambulacral vessels.

The main trunks of the ambulacral vessels consist of the circular vessel belonging to the disc and of the radial vessels issuing from it into the arms. The circular vessel (Tab. II, fig. 12 f) has its place in the circular groove or semi-canal which is situated on the skeleton of the disc (the bucal ring) round the interior wall and bounded below by the thickened edge whereto the bucal skin is attached. The periosteum-like tendinous membrane covering the ambulacral skeleton goes uninterrupted over this groove; so that the circular vessel thus becomes enveloped in a completely closed canal. On the side of this canal which is turned towards the perivisceral cavity, there appear a number of peculiar small globules (fig. 11, 12 d) which immediately attract the eye by their yellowish color. They are usually attached in pairs (more rarely 3 together) close below all the wedge-plates, and have the form of small thin-skinned vesicles (fig. 14) containing in their interior a finely granulated matter (fig. 13). Of the nature of these globules, which also occur in the same place in other Asteridæ, I can not state anything positively. According to their structure they might appear to form a sort of secretive apparatus. Of the ampolla-like enlargements of the annular vessel (the so-called Polish bladders) so strongly developed in other star-fishes, there is indeed no trace to be seen in the Brisinga; but I have reason to presume that they nevertheless really exist, and that the before mentioned rather wide cavities in the interior of the bucal ring, bounded by the parietal plate and the wedge-plate, are destined to receive such reservoirs of water for the circular vessel.

The radial ambulacral vessels, the number of which corresponds to that of the arms, issue from the circular vessel at right angles; traverse the groove wherein this vessel lies, and then extend along the ventral side of the disc and the arms, close in to the ambulacral skeleton, occupying a corresponding narrow groove, which runs along the whole arm at the bottom of the ventral furrow, and is partially covered over with a tendinous ligament. On account of its concealed position this vessel is very difficult to extract. It appears however very distinctly in all the sections of the arm (see Tab. III, fig. 3) as also on the exterior side of the isolated disc, where the arms have been attached (fig. 1 b). From these radial vessels there issue on each side, at short intervals, lateral canals, which supply the paired water-feet and their ampollæ with water.

b. The water-feet and their ampollæ.

The water-feet or ambulacral tentacles, which, as in other star-fishes, represent the most important locomotive organs of the animal, are very strongly developed, and are in structure and arrangement quite similar to those of other star-fishes. They issue in a similar manner from the bottom of the deep ventral furrows which run along the ventral side of the arms and the disc; and they are here arranged in a double row. At the base of each of them there is on the inside a large membranous bladder or ampolla protruding freely through the so-called ambulacral pores into the interior cavity of the arms, and forming along the upper side of the ambulacral skeleton a double row (see Tab. III. fig. 3 c. fig. 4 and 17). These ampollæ represent contractile reservoirs of water, by the help of which the water-feet can at any time be made to swell or to contract. Similar ampollæ are also observed projecting from the ambulacral pores (fig. 1 c) which correspond with the water-feet of the disc. When fully extended, the water-feet in the Brisinga are 2—3 times longer than the arm is broad, and they are curved and twisted in various manners (see Tab. I. fig. 12—14). Even in spirit-specimens they will always be found extended far beyond the ventral furrows, whence it seems evident that the water-feet in the Brisinga are not so highly contractile as those of other star-fishes. In form they are (see fig. 22) cylindro-conical or broadest at the base, tapering regularly towards the extremity, where they have a muscular circular suction disc. In the interior, these water-feet exhibit as usual a wide cavity filled with water; their exterior skin is interwoven with numerous close muscular fibres longitudinal as well as circular; but there is no trace of calcareous particles in the terminal disc, nor in any other part of the skin. The before mentioned double rows of water-feet, which extend along the whole ventral side of the arms, are also continued (see Tab. I. fig. 2) immediately on to the underside of the disc itself; so that there are for each arm 4 water-feet which specially belong to the disc. In a 10-armed specimen therefore the number of the water-feet belonging to the disc will be 40.

c. The madreporic body and the stone-canal.

The Madreporic body is in the Brisinga, as in the other star-fishes, situated on the dorsal side of the disc in the interval between 2 arms at their issue. It is however here, by reason of the small breadth of the skeleton of the disc, moved out quite towards the edge, where it covers the tubercular projecting upper end of one of the wedge-plates (see Tab. I, fig. 3, 4, 6 Tab. II, fig 1, 2, 8, 11, 12 a). It is in full grown specimens rather large, strongly convex, and of a more or less circular form. The surface is as usual very uneven, having numerous irregular narrow raised ribs, which radiate from a medial depression; but there is here in our present species not any trace of spines as in the Brisinga endecacnemos. From the madreporic body, the so-called *stone canal* (Tab. II, fig. 12 e) extends somewhat obliquely downwards along the interior wall of the bucal ring connecting itself with the circular ambulacral vessel (f). This so-called stone-canal is rather thin, but of a very firm consistency, on account of the numerous porous calcareous particles contained in it; its upper extremity is in great part covered by the wide cuticular sheath (c) which projects into the cavity of the disc and serves to envelope a very problematical organ, the so-called Heart, while its lower extremity lies quite free on one side of the sheath, and connects itself with the circular ambulacral vessel, after forming a small S-like curve. The water sucked in by the madreporic plate is still further filtered through the stone canal, and then conducted over to the annular vessel to be conveyed thence further into the radial water-vessels which run along the bottom of the ambulacral furrows of the arms.

4. The muscular System.

We have already several times had occasion to mention this system. In the Brisinga there are a very great number of muscles, but they are mostly very small, and of an extremely simple structure. Not only are all the single vertebræ or joints in the ambulacral skeleton of the arms movably connected together by short muscles going from one to the other in the periphery of the articulating surfaces of the single calcareous plates, but even every one of the spines situated along the sides of the arms and on the underside of the disc, is provided with such short muscles which move the spine in different directions; nay every single one of the microscopic pedicellariæ, which in immense numbers cover the cuticular sheaths of all the spines and the soft transversal ridges on the dorsal side of the arms, has, as already noticed, its special muscular apparatus. All these muscles seem however, as before stated, to be of extremely simple structure, and should properly be regarded merely as contractile ligaments, the smooth fibres of which are all parallel. But the muscular system seems to be more developed in the water-feet, and especially in the extremely contractile bucal membrane. Here we find several distinct layers of muscles, the fibres of which cross each other in different directions, and thereby bring about a more complete mobility of the said parts.

5. The nervous System.

In the nervous system we find again the same radial arrangement as has been already mentioned in reference to the ambulacral system. In the main features it corresponds completely with what we know in other Asteridæ. The chief parts, or the central parts, are formed by the ambulacral nerves belonging to the arms, or as we may call them the ambulacral brains. They have each (Tab. VI, fig. 1, 5) the form of a narrow band lying quite superficially, and extending along the middle of the ambulacral furrow in the whole length of the arm. In the middle this band forms a distinctly elevated ridge, arching over a narrow longitudinal canal or sinus which is divided by a medial septum (a) in two compartments. During its course it sends out on each side fine converging nerves to the water-feet, and in the spaces between the latter it expands on each side, insensibly merging in the cuticular lining. It terminates at the point of the arm in a somewhat claviform enlargement (fig. 12 b) which lies at the base of a peculiar organ of sense herein-after more particularly described. The whole nervous band is of a light yellowish color and is particularly brittle and fragile, lying so closely enveloped in the thin membrane which lines the ambulacral furrow, that it can only with extreme difficulty be dissected out and isolated from the adjacent parts. On removing the water-feet however, it may be distinctly perceived along the whole length of the ambulacral furrow. These nervous bands belonging to the arms are continued immediately inwards on the underside of the disc, where they likewise occupy the middle of the ambulacral furrow, and when the water-feet are removed, appear very distinctly (Tab. VI, fig. 1 b). At the interior extremity of the ambulacral furrows, all the ambulacral nerves are connected by a somewhat broader band-like circular commissure (ibid a) situated close in against the bucal ring at its junction with the bucal membrane. This commissure lies, like the ambulacral nervous band itself, quite superficially extending along the lower side of the circular rim which projects from the inner wall of the bucal ring, and it is, only at the end of the interradial spaces, partially covered over by the edges of the inner adambulacral plates with their diverging spines. Like the ambulacral nerves this commissure also seems to arch over a narrow circular sinus, which stands in connection with the above-mentioned radial canals running along the ventral furrows of the arms.

6. Organs of sense.

Under this category we must class a peculiar organ which is situated at the extreme point of all the arms. The organ exists there, as well in the previously observed form B.

endecacnemos as in the present species. That it has not been noticed before in the Brisinga, is owing to the extreme point of the arm being so easily broken off when the animal is taken. In a perfect arm the organ is always present, and easily distinguishable; the skeleton of the arm forming here a peculiar enlargement, covered with spines, and in the form of a somewhat bent plate, which is destined precisely to protect the organ in question. It is well known that in many star-fish there is at this place a very conspicuous red pigmentary spot, in which there has been noticed a peculiar structure of the extremities of the nerves completely answering to the so-called chrystal cones in the compound eyes of Articulata, for which reason these pigmentary spots have been confidently designated as real apparatus of vision. It was therefore reasonable to anticipate that we should find the organ under consideration in the Brisinga likewise adapted to serve in some manner as an organ of sight. Closer inspection has however not confirmed this presumption. The 2 essential parts which characterise the apparatus of sight in other Asteridæ, namely pigment and chrystal cones, are wanting. But it corresponds in its structure more with an other far less conspicuous part, situated close above the organ of sight, in the form of a simple tentacle, which in appearance is very little different from one of the ordinary water-feet, excepting that it is unpaired. In the Brisinga the organ in question (see Tab. II, fig. 5, 6 c, fig. 7 a) has the form of a soft cylindrical plug evenly rounded at the extremity, and of relatively considerable size, many times larger than the nearest very rudimentary water-feet; like these it is directed downwards; and it is sheltered as under a vaulted arch, by the before mentioned peculiar calcareous plate (see fig. 5) which is thickly covered with pedicellariæ. In its structure it seems on the whole to correspond pretty nearly with the water-feet. Like them it is hollow in the interior, and is filled with water from the ambulacral vessel. Its walls are rather thick, but seem to want the layers of muscle peculiar to the water-feet. At the extremity, it is surrounded by a thin transparent membrane a little raised from the proper wall, and here, a fine radial striation is observed. The structure of this organ is, as may be seen, very simple, and it might easily be taken for an unpaired water-foot, simply closing at this place the double row of these organs which runs along the ventral furrows of the arms, if its unusual size, its peculiar protection, and the evident enlargement of the ambulacral nerve at its base, did not indicate an entirely special function. It is for this reason that I must presume it to be an organ of sense. But what sort of sensation is transmitted through it, is difficult to say. It can scarcely be a pure and simple feeler, a mere tentacle. In this capacity the numerous water-feet far-reaching and movable in all directions might naturally be presumed to suffice; while on the other hand the isolated position, slight mobility, and peculiar protection of the organ here considered, would evidently make it less well adapted for such a function. Probably the animal receives through it a more specific conception of its surroundings than it receives by means of immediate contact; and we might perhaps rather be justified in regarding it as a sort of organ of smell analogous to the so-called olfactory papillæ in the Arthropods.

4*

7. The digestive System.

The digestive system in the Brisinga exhibits in its general structure the typical organisation of the proper star-fishes. We have to distinguish 1) The bucal aperture with its muscular apparatus, 2) the digestive cavity or stomach and 3) the radial cæca. We shall consider each of these principal parts separately.

a. The bucal aperture with its muscular apparatus (the bucal membrane).

In the middle of the under-side of the disc in the Brisinga, there appears a more or less wide or gaping circular opening, which is the mouth (Tab. I, fig. 2, 5 f, Tab. II, fig. 11 c). It is surrounded and limited by a naked membrane attached along the inner periphery of the skeleton of the disc (the bucal ring) to the circular projecting edge which is formed by the lower parts of the parietal plates. This bucal aperture is of a very variable appearance. It is sometimes quite small and narrow, only occupying the centre of the under-side of the disc, and far removed from the interior border of the skeleton; sometimes it is so much enlarged that it occupies nearly all the ventral space within the bucal ring, and thereby becomes apparently bounded only by the skeleton of the disc itself. Its form is also rather variable; as it is sometimes more irregularly shaped (see Tab. II, fig. 11) or drawn out in one direction or another, to an oval or elliptical shape (see Tab. I, fig. 2). This variability in size and form of the bucal aperture, depends on the great contractility of the membrane which limits it (the bucal membrane). On closer examination it will also be found that this membrane (Tab. II, fig. 11 b) is interwoven by a complicated system of fine muscular fibres which have partly a radial and partly a circular arrangement. The radial fibres diverge from the border of the mouth, which often exhibits an extremely fine crenulation (see Tab. II, fig. 11) and attach themselves round about to the skeleton of the disc. By the action of these fibres, the bucal membrane can be contracted from all sides; the consequence of which will be, that the bucal aperture will be enlarged. The circular fibres act antagonistically; as they contribute together, like a sphincter, to restrict the bucal aperture and thus extend the bucal membrane. Also in other star-fishes, there is a similar bucal membrane; but it is so little developed that the bucal aperture seems to be limited directly by the intruding angles of the skeleton of the disc with the spines on the same: these spines are often of a peculiar form, and have therefore been distinguished by the appellation bucal spines; they may indeed also act partly, as a sort of masticatory apparatus. If we imagine in the Brisinga the bucal membrane in its highest degree of contraction, whereby consequently the bucal aperture will occupy the whole of the ventral space within the bucal ring; then the ends of the interradial spaces formed by the adambulacral plates of the interior vertebræ will make the limits of the mouth; and the spines diverging inwards from these plates in fan-like fascicles may also partly be able to act as bucal spines; for which reason we have also thus named them in the foregoing.

b. The digestive cavity.

Through the more or less gaping bucal aperture in the Brisinga, there is an uninterrupted view into the digestive cavity (Tab. 1, fig. 2 & 5) which occupies the greatest part of the cavity of the disc. Its walls form below the immediate continuation of the bucal membrane, as the latter (see Tab. II, fig. 9 b) suddenly curves itself round outwards at the border of the bucal aperture, acquiring at the same time a different quality and structure. There is thus no proper section which might be compared to the æsophagus; and immediately within the border of the mouth the digestive cavity or stomach begins. It has the form of a flat and wide sack, the walls of which are tolerably thick, and consist of 2 distinct layers: an outer fibrous, and an inner cellular, which latter forms numerous irregular folds and sinuosities projecting inwards (see fig. 9). The exterior convex surface of the stomach, which likewise exhibits a more or less well defined longitudinal folding, is attached to the bucal ring by numerous very strong fine tendinous fibres (fig. 9 a). These tendinous fibres, which form an immediate continuation of the tendinous membrane that covers the skeleton of the disc, issue (see fig. 11 c) close together from the upper edge of the latter, just before the insertion of the arms; that is from the dorsal side of the ambulacral plates of the interior vertebræ; they extend themselves horisontally inwards, diverging from each other, and attach themselves at the same height, round the exterior wall of the stomach.

The stomach is moreover fastened in the middle to the dorsal skin of the disc, by a central ligament which will be hereafter described. By this ligament, and by the tendinous fibres before mentioned, the stomach is thus kept in its place and, as it were, suspended in the central cavity which it fills almost entirely; only leaving below a very small space, like a canal surrounding the lower part of the stomach, limited below by the upper surface of the bucal membrane, and on the outside by the interior wall of the bucal ring. This space, thus representing the lower part of the perivisceral cavity, stands round the periphery in connexion with a similar narrow upper space, which above the radial spaces of the bucal ring, communicates again with the cavities of the arms.

The upper part of the stomach is separated, by a distinctly marked annular fold, from the lower proper digestive cavity, with which it nevertheless communicates by a wide circular aperture. From the periphery of this narrow upper section of the alimentary cavity there radiate (see Tab. II, fig. 8 c and fig. 10) on all sides the strongly developed so-called radial cæca, hereafter more particularly described, extending far into the cavities of the arms.

The upper wall of this section, which thus forms properly the bottom of the digestive cavity, and can also be seen more or less completely through the gaping bucal aperture (see Tab. 1, fig. 2, 5 f) has the form of a flat extended circular disc of half the diameter of the proper stomach. Its structure seems to be very peculiar. On the interior or lower side turned towards the digestive cavity, it exhibits (see Tab. II, fig. 10) an appearance of being, as it were, granulated, having on its surface numerous small wart-like elevations or sinuosities of a glandular structure, which, especially towards the centre, are crowded together and projecting, and in this part frequently arranged in larger or smaller groups separated by more or less distinct sinuous furrows; towards the periphery these elevations become more indistinct, and disappear at last entirely where the radial cæca take their issue. The upper side (see Tab. II, fig. 8 e) which is in great part covered by a glandular apparatus (f) attached here in the centre, (hereafter more particularly noticed) seems to exhibit an entirely different structure. We remark here a very conspicuous and peculiar striation, which on closer examination appears like a number of raised ribs radiating from the centre to the periphery and divided by intermediary furrows into a great many finer and finer ramifications. The whole has at the first glance a striking resemblance to a ramified complicated system of canals in the walls of the digestive cavity; and a corresponding structure in other starfishes seems also to have been considered by an earlier naturalist (Tidemann) as a part of the supposed blood-vessel system (stomach veins). Nevertheless on more minute investigation, and especially by examining the transverse section of this part, the conviction is soon acquired that here is no real system of canals, but only a peculiar radial corrugation of the roof of the digestive cavity itself, which only appears distinctly on the upper side of the same; while on the lower side it is completely hidden by the numerous wart-like papillæ projecting in the digestive cavity.

I have not been able to find any evident central aperture in the upper wall. The whole digestive cavity appears to be quite closed, without any part being discoverable that can properly be called an intestine. There may indeed be remarked on the outside of the dorsal skin of the disc a fine opening or pore (Tab. 1, fig. 4, 7 a) which according to its position might easily be taken for an anal aperture; but I consider it certain that this is not the case. It is, as will be shewn in the sequel, only the exterior outlet for a strongly developed glandular organ which has its place in the middle between the stomach and the dorsal skin, and which answers to the so-called interradial cæca in other star-fishes.

c. The radial cæca.

These organs, which are peculiar to the proper star-fish and entirely wanting in the Ophiuræ, and which must be considered as special sections of the digestive cavity destined for the individual arms, are also very distinctly developed in the Brisinga. Even if they do not, as in other star-fishes, extend right into the points of the arms, they are yet in proportion to the central part of the digestive cavity situated in the disc, at least quite as strongly developed as in the others, extending about to the end of the 1st third part of the arms, and are thus more than 4 times as long as the diameter of the disc (see Tab. VI, fig. 35). They take their issue as single rather wide and somewhat flattened tubes in the periphery of the upper section of the stomach (see Tab. II, fig. 8 c c, fig. 10) and radiate thence on all sides, extending horisontally over the lower folded section of the stomach and over the ambulacral plates of the disc into the cavities of the arms. Immediately on entering into the arms, they divide themselves fork-like into 2 main trunks (see Tab. II, fig. 8 c on the right; Tab. III, fig. 25 a) which then run side by side in a tolerably straight direction along the dorsal side of the arms. On each side, these main trunks send out short and closely placed thin-skinned lobes or secondary cæca, variously folded and contorted, giving to the whole organ an elegant ramified appearance. The radial cæca, the number of which will thus correspond with that of the arms, are firmly attached to the inside of the dorsal skin in their whole extent by 2 longitudinal parallel ligaments. At a short distance from the issue of the radial cæca from the stomach, each of these ligaments is connected with the adjacent one by a thin arched commissure which is likewise firmly attached to the dorsal skin. Then they separate themselves from this skin, and follow the radial cæca to their issue from the stomach, going over into the upper wall of the latter, after having again connected themselves with their neighbors by a thin membrane, which on the outside is deeply concave. The stomach is hereby as it were suspended from the dorsal skin by a sort of rather complicated mesentery pierced at the angles between the issues of the radial cæca, by large semilunar apertures, through which the central space between the roof of the digestive cavity and the dorsal skin communicates with the other perivisceral cavity (see Tab. VI. fig. 6).

The fluid contained in the cavities of the radial cæca is of a more or less clear yellowish color, and contains a considerable quantity of fat or oil which collects itself in larger or smaller bubbles on the surface of the water, when the cæca are opened and the contents allowed to flow out.

8. The perivisceral cavity (cæloma) and the Blood system.

The cavity, immediately limited by the skin and the interior skeleton, which contains the various viscera, is in the Brisinga well developed; and it is not, as in the Ophiuræ, only restricted to the disc, but extends also, as in the proper star-fishes, into the arms and even to their extreme points. In the basal section of the arms, it is (see Tab. III, fig. 3) very wide; so that besides the radial cæca (d d) it can here contain also the frequently very strongly developed organs of generation (e e). In the periphery of the disc, the cavities of the arms are by a proportionally very narrow aperture connected with the cavity of the disc, which uninterruptedly surrounds the central part of the digestive cavity or stomach, without being here, as in other star-fishes, divided by radial septa into several distinct spaces. The whole perivisceral cavity is, as already mentioned, filled with an aquæous fluid which thus immediately surrounds the interior organs. This fluid is however, as has also been shewn in the case of other star-fishes, not purely and simply water, but contains also numerous small cellular elements freely suspended in the same. According to their whole nature, these cellular elements are real blood globules; and the said fluid must therefore, even if mixed with considerable quantities of water taken in from without, be considered as real blood. The whole perivisceral cavity represents therefore in the Brisinga — and as I must presume also in the other star-fishes, one single great reservoir of blood.

I have not succeeded, even with the utmost attention, in discovering any actual blood vessels in the Brisinga; not to speak of the complicated system of veins and arteries which, according to the indications of earlier naturalists, is said to be found in some star-fishes. I have endeavored, by repeated dissections and preparations, to discover in the Brisinga the widely ramified dorsal or venous system of blood vessels so minutely described by Tiedemann, but always without any result. Whatever may at first have appeared to resemble such a system has always, when more closely examined, shewn itself to be something quite different: namely sometimes the ligaments and tendinous fibres whereby the interior organs, and especially those of the digestive system, are attached to the dorsal skin, sometimes a peculiar folding in the walls of these organs. Neither have I been able to confirm the observations of the earlier naturalists with respect to the ventral or arterial system of blood vessels. Real blood vessels are indeed not to be discovered here, but only a narrow longitudinal canal-like sinus, without any special walls, extending along the ventral furrows of the arms, immediately above the radial nerve-bands, and communicating with a similar narrow circular sinus enclosed between the 2 lamellæ of the bucal cuticle nearest to the bucal ring. My investigations of other native star-fishes have given the same negative result. Real blood vessels are no where to be found; according to which I must suppose that the earlier representations of the blood system of star-fish are inaccurate and founded on a less careful examination. There is however one part that has been likewise referred by earlier naturalists to the blood-vessel-system, and which is very distinctly developed and strongly prominent in the Brisinga, that is namely the peculiar membranous organ which in other star-fishes extends from the ventral to the dorsal wall of the disc accompanying the stone-canal in its whole course, which is usually regarded as the central organ of circulation or heart, whereby the supposed ventral (arterial) and the dorsal (venous) circular vessels are said to be connected. This organ lies, as we know, in other star-fishes together with the stone-canal enclosed between the double lamellæ of one of the radial septa which divide the cæloma of the disc like a fan. As there are no such radial septa in the Brisinga, the organ is here enclosed and kept in position by a sheath-like duplicature of the tendinous membrane which lines the inside of the skeleton of the disc, and thereby firmly attached to the interior wall of the bucal ring. When the stomach is removed, the said sheath appears (Tab. II, fig. 11, 12 c) like a short and thick pillar projecting convexly inwards and extending vertically along the interior wall of the bucal ring, connecting the bucal membrane with the dorsal cuticle of the disc at the place where the madreporic body (a) is situated; it also partly incloses the upper end of the stone-canal (c). On cutting through the exterior tendinous skin, the membranous organ in question (comp. Tab. VI, fig 6 h & fig. 8) will immediately be discovered partly attached on the upper side by a ligament to the stone-canal (s), and with its upper end attached to the dorsal skin at the same height as the stone-canal, but somewhat inside or on the inner edge of the madreporic body. Its other extremity extends considerably further downwards than the stone-canal, curving itself round the thickened edge of the bucal ring, which below bounds the half-canal or duct wherein the circular ambulacral vessel is situated. The organ is here attached by a broad base to the skeleton of the disc. With regard to the more particular structure of the organ, it appears (fig. 8) like a membranous tube variously folded and contorted; its walls exhibit under the microscope (see fig. 9) a fine net-like structure; thickened and thin places alternating with each other. There may be plainly perceived in them light longitudinal fascicles of fibres, partly anastomosing with each other and surrounded by a more opaque fine granular tissue. In spirit specimens, the walls of the tube will usually be found collapsed or in contact with each other; but in fresh specimens, this does not seem to be the case. In the interior of it is found a fluid, which appears to be of the same nature as that contained in the perivisceral cavity. The connexion of the upper part of the tube with the dorsal skin might justify the assumption that it here terminates blindly. I have however reason to suppose that there may yet be found here a sort of communication with the perivisceral cavity; although I have not yet succeeded in indicating any such communication with certainty. The lower end of the tube lies close to the before mentioned circular sinus, which is inclosed between the 2 lamellæ of the bucal cuticle; and the tube stands here, as I believe, in free communication with the sinus.

Having as already mentioned, not been able to demonstrate any real ventral or dorsal system of blood-vessels, nor to find in the Brisinga any special organs of respiration which could make such a distinction of arteries and veins probable, I cannot attribute to this apparatus the importance which has been ascribed to it. In any case it appears to me that many circumstances forbid the assumption that we have here the real central organ for the circulation of the blood. Of the probable distination of the organ I shall say something more in a subsequent section (Physiology).

9. Organs of secretion.

Under this category may be reckoned a rather voluminous and according to its whole structure exquisite glandular apparatus (Tab. II, fig. 8 f g) which has its place in the middle, immediately above the roof of the stomach between it and the dorsal skin of the disc. The apparatus, which evidently enough corresponds according to its situation to the so-called interradial cæca or rectal cæca in other star-fishes, consists of 2 unequal parts united in the middle, of which one is usually twice as large as the other. Their arrangement is always constant, so that the smaller section turns to that side of the periphery where the madreporic body is situated, but their size varies in different individuals. In the middle, where both sections unite, the whole apparatus is attached by a ligament, as well to the roof of the stomach as to the inside of the dorsal cuticle, on which the ligament is continued in the form of 2 thickened stripes proceeding from the centre in different directions, and then both curving towards one side of the periphery, uniting themselves each with one of the longitudinal ligaments by which the 2 radial cæca situated nearest on the right of the madreporic body are attached (see Tab. VI, fig. 6). The central part of the ligament is perforated by a narrow canal, the excretory passage, which ascends and has its issue on the dorsal side of the disc in a fine pore surrounded by a somewhat raised elliptical border (Tab. I, fig. 1 a). Although the point where the ligament is attached to the inside of the dorsal skin lies exactly in the centre, it will always be found that the said pore has an evidently excentric position, being always found nearer to that side of the periphery where the madreporic body has its place (see Tab. I, fig. 3, 4 a. Tab. II. fig. 1, 2). This is caused by the excretory passage perforating the thick dorsal skin in a very oblique direction, which also quite naturally accounts for the peculiar elliptical form of this pore (Tab. I, fig. 7 a).

With respect to the structure of the apparatus in question, it seems to be, as before mentioned, completely glandulous. Both the main parts which compose the apparatus consist of a rather firm and compact mass externally divided into a greater or less number of large irregular lobes, and each of these lobes again into a great number of smaller rounded lobules, whereby the whole apparatus acquires the appearance of a real acinous gland. On the outside there is a thin but tolerably resistent membrane, wherein there may be seen, more or less distinctly, various fibres that partly cross each other (muscular fibres), and inside an opaque white granular substance, which on the side where both sections meet appears more loose and transparent. The whole apparatus rests immediately on the roof of the stomach, but so that a greater or smaller part of the latter always remains uncovered (see Tab. II. fig. 8).

10. Organs of Generation.

In full grown specimens we often find, as before mentioned, that the arms at some distance from the base exhibit a very remarkably strong enlargement; the dorsal skin rising high above the subjacent ambulacral skeleton, while it otherwise lies more or less closely on the same (Tab. I, fig. 12. Tab. II, fig. 1). On slitting the skin it will be found that the cavity of the arms (coelom) is here stretched by a very voluminous mass divided into numerous lobes and branches, which in different individuals exhibit a somewhat different appearance. This mass represents the organs of generation, which in some individuals appear as ovaries and in others as spermaries. Both sorts of organs of generation are easily distinguished from each other, partly by the color and partly by the manner of ramification; but else they occupy the same place in the cavity of the arms, without ever extending into the coelom of the disc. By spreading on each side the dorsal skin when slit in the middle, and pushing asunder the various lobes or ramifications from each other (see Tab. III, fig. 4, 17) it is easy to ascertain that what appeared at first glance to be a confused mass of lobes, belongs to 2 organs, lying symmetrically on each side of the medial line, each of which is attached only by one point to the interior of the skin. On examining the skin at this place more closely, an evident exterior opening will be discovered (see Tab. I, fig. 12 a, Tab. III, fig. 25 c c) surrounded by tuberous projecting borders, which is the issue for the sexual products. These exterior apertures for generation are usually situated quite symmetrically, one on each side of the arm nearer to the lower side, and distant about one diameter of the disc from the base of the arm. When once their position has been noticed, it will never afterwards be difficult to find them on any arm, without proceeding to any dissection.

a. The Ovaries.

The ovaries have usually (see Tab. III, fig. 4) the form of more or less elongated and ramified cylindrical tubes which at last unite themselves on each side to a common short trunk attached to the inside of the skin and containing the short exit passage (oviduct) through which the mature ova are ejected from the body. Sometimes several such ovarian tubes are blended together in the form of large irregular sack-like enlargements, whereby the whole ovary acquires a more crowded and compact appearance (see fig. 5, 6). These enlargements may then either begin with ovarian tubes in the usual form (fig. 7) or they may exhibit only small rounded lobes (fig. 8) or even only form simply rounded reservoirs (see fig. 5). Even in the smallest specimens I have been able to examine, I have found

36

evident incipient ovaries in the usual place. Notwithstanding their small size, they exhibited already distinctly their characteristic form and ramification (see fig. 9, 10). The fully developed ovaries are of a more or less intense reddish yellow color, and are already hereby immediately distinguishable from the spermaries, which are always of a lighter whitish color. The skin which surrounds the various ovarian tubes is rather firm, fibrous and semitransparent; so that the ova-cells inside may be seen through them more or less distinctly (see fig. 4, 11).

On examining the contents of such a tube, there will be found egg-cells very differently developed. The smallest of them (fig. 12, 13), which can only with difficulty be distinguished from the epithelial cells that line the inside of the wall of the tube, are perfectly pellucid, often of an irregular form, and without any distinct exterior membrane, but all furnished with a large and well defined nucleus (germinative vesicle) wherein there may usually be distinguished a single small nucleolus (germinative point). The larger egg-cells (fig. 14, 15) appear more isolated in the interior of the tube, and are sometimes quite detached from the walls. In them there may already be discerned a distinct light enveloping membrane (corion) and a greater or smaller quantity of reddish yellow yolk deposited in the cell-plasma, which makes them less transparent. Finally in the largest egg-cells (fig. 16) which always lie completely free in the interior of the ovarian tubes, this mass of yolk has increased so much, that the whole egg-cell, with exception of the clear enveloping membrane, becomes quite untransparent, and the germinative vesicle is usually quite hidden. In this state the egg seems to have arrived at maturity, and is then carried out by the ovarian ducts.

b. The spermaries (testes).

The spermaries (fig. 17, 18, 19) correspond, in their general form and arrangement on the whole, to the ovaries; but are easily distinguished from the latter by their lighter whitish color, and by the single tubes or cæca not being simply cylindrical, but in many ways bent and lobed, whereby the whole organ exhibits a still more complicated appearance than the ovaries. In young specimens (see fig. 18, 20) the single cæca may usually be traced in their whole length, as narrow tubes nearly of uniform thickness, but bent in and out at short intervals or zig-zagged, and gradually uniting themselves to a certain number of converging main-trunks. These are at last connected in a single short exit, which issues at the same place as the ovaries in the females (fig. 19 a). In older specimens the single cæca often form (see fig. 17) as is the case with the ovaries, large sack-like enlargements, which externally exhibit innumerable small rounded lobes. If one of the extremities of the cæca is viewed under a microscope, it will be found (see fig. 21) that their interior is, as it were, divided into a number of irregular spaces, wherein are found numerous small clear elliptic bodies with a great number of interior nuclei. These bodies (fig. 22) represent the developing cells of the spermatozoa. In the larger sack-like extensions we find the fully developed spermatozoa, which lie here together in large clusters or heaps (see fig. 25). The single spermatozoa consist (fig. 24) of two sharply distinguished parts, head and tail. The head is more or less globular, completely pellucid, and contains one or more clear nuclei. The so-called tail, which can often attain a very considerable length, has the form of an extremely fine thread or bristle. I could not discover any independent undulating movement in them. But there was during the dissection an evident constant movement of the whole mass of semen, probably caused by the elastic tails or bristles of the spermatozoa gradually straightening themselves out from their original convolved position.

IV

General arrangement of the various organic systems.
(Topography).

If the various organs described in the foregoing lines are considered in connexion with each other, we shall find that each arm (antimeron) contains in itself all the most important organic systems (vital organs). In the disc these organic systems are so connected that the whole complex of arms forms a common organism. We have thus in fact in the single arm a complete expression for the whole organisation. The complete star-fish is in other words to be considered as a multiple of arms or rays arranged around a common centre and (in the disc) brought into organic connexion with each other. In the disc we find therefore chiefly connecting parts (commissures) between the various organic systems of the arms; while the real principal parts of the organs have their place in the arms themselves. To enumerate separately the particular organic systems above noticed: the commissure of the ambulacral skeleton is formed by the so-called oral ring, or, (as the ambulacral vertebræ contained in the same are flush with the skeleton of the arm, and in reality represent the interior continuation of the same) more correctly speaking, only by the connecting plates peculiar to the disc viz. the wedge-plates and the parietal plates; the commissure of the cuticular system is formed by the dorsal skin of the disc; the commissure of the water system, by the circular ambulacral vessel; the commissure of the nervous system by the circular nervous band lying in the periphery of the oral cuticle; the commissure of the digestive system, by the central stomach, with its single oral aperture; the commissure of the blood-system, by the cavity of the disc surrounding the stomach and by the circular blood-sinus contained between the lamellæ of the oral cuticle.

The special organic systems of the disc are only the apparatus of secretion and the so-called „heart", if we do not reckon this last as belonging to the blood-system.

The special organs of the arms are the organs of generation and the terminal organ of sense.

The foundation of each single arm consists again of a series of similar consecutive joints or metamera, each of which contains its own section of the skeleton, water-vessel, nervous and muscular systems, with a corresponding pair of external members (water-feet,

The terminal joint of the arm is however distinguished, as stated, from the others by a remarkable development, and by the absence of water-feet, in stead of which it is furnished with the above-noticed special organ of sense. This joint is, as will be shewn hereafter, the oldest of them all; and it is from the basis of this that all the others develop themselves little by litle during the growth of the arm. There is a common cuticle for all the metamera and a common blood-cavity. Of the interior organs contained in the latter, the digestive system (the radial cæca) is limited to the basal third part of the arm; and the organs of generation are limited only to a certain section of this last part.

If we now endeavor to picture to ourselves the manner in which these different organic systems are topographically arranged in relation to each other, we shall obtain the best view by examining a section of an arm. If we take this in the basal part, and at the place where the organs of generation are situated, we shall find all the most important organs of the arm in the section and in their relative positions, (see Tab. III, fig. 3). Above and on the sides there appears the highly convex dorsal cuticle with its 2 layers: on the outside, the soft epidermoidal layer with its pedicellariæ; on the inside, the fibrous layer with the calcareous ribs contained therein, from which rise the spines ranged in circlets along the same with their cuticular sheaths formed by the epidermis. Limited above and on the sides immediately by the cuticle, appears the perivisceral cavity or the blood-cavity with the interior organs inclosed; highest up and intimately connected with the inside of the cuticle, the double radial cæca (d d) with their lateral sinuosities; further down and on the sides, the well developed organs of generation (e e) which here fill the greater part of the perivisceral cavity, with their numerous ramified cæca; below, and here limiting the perivisceral cavity, appears the ambulacral skeleton (b) with the dorsal ridge (projecting upwards in the middle into the interior of the arm), on the sides of which ridge the thin-skinned ampollæ (c) for the water-feet project from the ambulacral pores. The ambulacral skeleton is connected on each side with the dorsal cuticle, and thus closes completely the cavity of the arm below; the long marginal spines (f f) project externally at this place on each side. Immediately below the ambulacral skeleton, at the bottom of the ventral furrow formed by the same, there appears in the middle a narrow opening (see fig. 1 b) which is the section of the radial ambulacral vessel; this opening is in the lower part separated by transversal ligaments from another narrow opening (fig. 1 a) which represents the radial blood-sinus; this last is again covered by the band-shaped radial nerve, which nerve again is covered by the thin membrane lining the ventral furrow and going over at the sides immediately into the tendinous cuticle which clothes the ambulacral skeleton. From the bottom of the ambulacral furrow there project to a greater or less distance the 2 water-feet (fig. 3 a) and from the adambulacral plates which limit the ventral furrow on the sides, there issue in various directions the so-called furrow-spines.

By examination of a section of the disc (see Tab. VI, fig. 3a) we may ascertain that the various connecting parts of the organic systems have on the whole a similar arrangement. In the lower part of the interior wall of the oral ring, we shall thus find the section of the circular ambulacral vessel, of the circular blood-sinus and of the commissure of the nerves, arranged precisely in the same manner and in the same serial order. In the middle of the disc, we have a longitudinal section of the central part of the digestive apparatus extended freely in the cavity of the disc: in the lower part, the oral aperture (m), limited by the horisontal naked oral membrane and leading immediately to the lower strongly corrugated section of the stomach (st), the periphery of which lies close in to the upper margin of the oral ring and is attached to it by fine tendinous fibres; above this section is the much narrower upper division of the stomach, which in its periphery is suspended by ligaments from the dorsal cuticle, and the cavity of which goes over on the sides into the radial cæca (r). Above the roof of the stomach, there appears finally in the centre the apparatus of secretion (n) with its short exit-duct issuing on the dorsal side of the disc. If the section is carried exactly through the interradial space in which the madreporic body is located, we have at the same time a longitudinal section of the latter (m) and of the two asymetrical parts standing in connexion with it, the stone-canal and the so-called heart (h). The oral ring (m r) will then on this side be cut through, so that the wedge plate will be bisected, and the 2 contiguous dorsal marginal plates, the 2 contiguous parietal plates and 2 pairs of contiguous adambulacral plates, will be separated from their connexion with each other. Immediately below the cut wedge-plate, the triangular cavity which exists in the interior of the oral ring at this part will appear. If the section is made on the opposite side of the oral ring precisely in a radial space, the oral ring will here be cut, so that the 2 ambulacral vertebræ corresponding to one arm will be longitudinally bisected; the section will thus coincide with the vertical sutures between the 2 pairs of ambulacral plates belonging to these vertebræ: and at the lower side (the bottom of the ventral furrow) we shall have a longitudinal section of the radial ambulacral vessel, of the radial blood-sinus and of the radial nerve. If we now consider an arm here in connexion with the disc, the skeleton of the latter will also be divided in the same manner; so that the consecutive vertebræ of the arm will all be bisected in the vertical sutures between the ambulacral plates.

V.

The vital functions.

(Physiology).

I. The animal functions.

It is of course very difficult to acquire any complete idea of these vital functions in the Brisinga; because the animal, by being brought up from the enormous depth at which it lives, is evidently placed in very abnormal exterior circumstances which must necessarily have a highly obstructive influence on such functions. But as I have been able to preserve specimens, or rather those parts of which the specimens consist, alive some time after capture, I have still succeeded in making a few observations on this subject which may not perhaps be without interest.

A. Movement.

The principal acting parts during the locomotion of the animal are certainly, as in other star-fishes, the numerous water-feet situated along the ventral furrows, by help of which the animal creeps slowly along the bottom in different directions. I have not however been able directly to observe the animal's true locomotion; and that for the very natural reason, that in all the specimens, as has been said, the arms have been at the time of capture more or less completely detached from the disc.

However in the arms thus separated one may see, as in other star-fishes, that the feet move in different manners, now contracting now extending themselves and turning in various directions, partly also attaching themselves by their suction-discs to the objects with which they come in contact. This changing play of the water-feet seems however in the Brisinga to be far from taking place with that liveliness and intensity that we have occasion to observe in other star-fishes, for instance in the genus Asterias; while we must not omit to allow for the abnormal circumstances in which the captured specimens of the Brisinga will always find themselves. As regards the proper movement of the water-feet, it is effected

6

apparently only by help of the muscles imbedded in their walls; not as is usually supposed by any independent contraction of the ampollæ belonging to the water-feet. These ampollæ are in any case in the Brisinga so extraordinarily thin-skinned, that they scarcely could have any other destination than to take up the superfluous water as simple reservoirs when the water-feet are contracted, and again to deliver out the water required when the water-feet are extended.

I have not been able directly to observe any independent movement of the arm-spines; but according to the frequently very different direction which they, especially the long marginal spines, shew in the captured specimens, sometimes standing out from the arm at nearly right angles, sometimes lying close to the sides of the arms, we may conclude that they really have a voluntary movement; an inference that seems also to be warranted by their peculiar articulation to the skeleton, and by the muscular skin surrounding their base.

Also the whole arm is to a certain extent movable: all the ambulacral vertebræ being, as already mentioned, movably connected with each other by elastic muscular ligaments. This movement, which is easily observed in the specimens recently captured, can take place both in a horizontal and in a vertical direction. In the last named movement the whole arm can even be curved upward nearly in a complete circle. The first named movement is chiefly observed in the exterior part of the arm only. All these movements of the arm are however far from being effected with the same force and rapidity as in the Ophiuræ, but in an extremely slow nearly imperceptible manner; it must however be remarked that in all probability all the movements, and consequently also these, would, while the animal is creeping on the bottom in its normal state, be effected with greater liveliness than noticed in the captured specimens. The greatest mobility seemed to exist between the exterior arm-joints; for which reason it is also especially this part of the arm which will be found variously bent and twisted, in the captured specimens. Nearer to the base the mobility becomes more and more limited, owing to the much shorter muscular ligaments between the single vertebræ, until, at the junction of the arm with the disc, it is nearly reduced to nothing. I have therefore reason to presume, that in the normal state the basal parts of the arm always retain unaltered their relative positions during the movements of the animal. When the animal is captured, and I think also in another case which will be subsequently noticed, an abnormal convulsive movement of the whole arm takes place, which causes the complete separation of the arm from the disc. Such a separation, always taking place just where the first vertebra of the arm connects itself with the immovable skeleton of the disc, may easily be explained, partly by the movement of the whole arm operating just at that point with the greatest force, and partly by the skin at that part being more easily broken than at any other.

Any movement of the disc itself is however made impossible by the firm attachment of the calcareous pieces composing the bucal ring. It is only in the softer parts, stretched within the calcareous ring, that phenomena of movement can be observed. Apart from the internal organs, these movements consist indeed in an essentially passive rising and sinking of the dorsal skin, accordingly as the fluid contained in the perivisceral cavity is more concentrated in the cavity of the disc or in that of the arms, whereby the roof of the disc becomes alternately rather convex or vaulted, and then quite flat again; moreover there is a contraction and extension of the bucal membrane, which takes place within very wide limits, and whereby the form and size of the bucal aperture can be materially altered.

B. Sensation.

I have already described as true instruments of sense the peculiar terminal organs of the arms (Tab. II, fig. 5, 6 c, fig. 7 a) the structure and peculiar protection of which distinguish them from all the other appendages of the body. I have previously developed my reasons for not supposing them to be simply and solely organs of feeling or tentacles. Although it is of course very difficult to decide as to the nature of the sensation received through these organs, there is however reason to presume that it must be of a more specific sort than the more indifferent sensation of feeling. If I have been disposed to consider them as something like organs of smell, it was only because in their structure they seemed to me to correspond to what in other invertebrate animals are usually called olfactory papillæ, but I do not therefore mean to say that the sensation conveyed through these organs must exactly correspond to what we understand by smell. There is naturally no objection to our assuming that in several of the lower animals there may be senses of an intermediate sort impossible to class precisely as any of the 5 human senses. With regard to the position of these organs of sense in the Brisinga, is is evident that in occupying the extreme point of the arms they have got the most convenient place which they could have had. The animal is hereby enabled to explore the immediate environs in all directions at the same time, and indeed over a very considerable area (more than 4 square feet); and whether the presence of suitable food or of inconvenience or danger be thus discerned, the animal will easily receive information through one or other of these organs and regulate its movements accordingly.

As real organs of feeling or tentacles (exclusively of their functions as organs of locomotion previously noticed) we must undoubtedly consider the numerous water-feet attached along the ambulacral furrows, which by their great contractility and mobility in all directions, and by their fine cuticular covering, seem to be admirably adapted for their functions in such capacity. All naturalists are also agreed in attributing both the functions mentioned to these organs in other star-fishes.

It is also extremely probable that the general cuticular covering, and especially the exterior layer of skin in the Brisinga, may be susceptible of a rather fine sensation of a more general kind.

C. Functions of the Pedicellariæ.

With regard to the nature and destination of these remarkable small organs, which, as is well known, are only peculiar to the proper star-fishes and to the Echinidæ, and which in the Brisinga exhibit a remarkably complicated structure, appearing also in greater number than in any other known Echinoderm, many and various conjectures have been set forth, without apparently elucidating their homology or their functions. Without flattering myself that I can solve the difficult problem in a perfectly satisfactory manner, I think that I ought here to set forth my views as to the latter point. The homology of the pedicellariæ will be noticed more particularly in a subsequent section.

From the structure of the pedicellariæ it may certainly be inferred that they are destined to seize and hold fast the objects which come in contact with them. Whether however the intention is to protect the tender and sensitive exterior cuticle, or to retain such particles as may serve the animal for food, is a question about which the opinions of the authors do not yet quite agree. In the Echinidæ it has certainly been ascertained, by direct observations on the living animal, that the pedicellariæ play an important part in removing the excrements expelled from the anal aperture, which else might easily become entangled among the numerous spines and thereby hinder the free play of the water-feet, and also pollute the fine layer of skin between the spines. For this purpose, only the pedicellariæ situated in the upper half of the shell are required. But pedicellariæ in just as great abundance are found also on the lower side of the shell, close up to the nearest environs of the mouth, where they even appear in quite unusual numbers. These pedicellariæ must certainly have a widely different destination in the economy of the animal. It is here in my opinion most natural to think of a retention of such particles as should serve for food, and which probably would be brought within reach of the mouth in a manner similar to that in which the excrements on the other side are conveyed away down the sides of the shell.

A similar difference in the pedicellariæ' functions may in my opinion also be presumed to exist in the Brisinga. The pedicellariæ situated on the dorsal side of the body and especially on the numerous soft transverse ridges of the arms, are probably chiefly intended for the removal from the dorsal surface of various extraneous matter (particles of mud &c) which might come in contact with them; thereby protecting the interjacent naked cuticle. But on the whole, we must certainly presume that those pedicellariæ have a different destination, which are found in masses on the cuticular sheaths of the spines, attached to the skeleton of the arms and of the disc, especially those at the extreme ends of the same.

We might indeed imagine, as regards the innermost furrow-spines, that the pedicellariæ attached to them were intended to prevent extraneous particles from penetrating and irritating the thin sensitive skin which covers the ambulacral furrows; and according to

45

the position and direction of these innermost furrow-spines, in between the far extending water-feet, this is also in a high degree probable. But such cannot be supposed to be the intention of the pedicellariae attached to the other spines. I presume on the contrary that their function, like that of the pedicellariae on the lower part of the shell of the Echinidæ, is principally exercised in the service of alimentation. If we consider a perfect arm (see Tab. II, fig. 1 & 2) it will be seen that these spines form together a broad brim extending along the sides of the arms from their basis to the extreme point. The width of the space hereby occupied, namely from the point of the marginal spines on one side to the corresponding point of the spines on the other side becomes as much as 6 times that of the arm itself; and consequently so much greater an area is commanded by the animal than if the spines were away. Now as soon as any particle of matter comes within reach of these spines, it is retained by the numerous pedicellariae situated on them; and at the same time the animal no doubt becomes aware of its presence. How far the particle of matter retained may be serviceable for the nourishment of the animal or not, may be probably more particularly investigated by the sensitive and flexible water-feet, which are extensible on all sides. In the latter case the object is rejected and removed; but in the former it must necessarily be brought within reach of the mouth. This may be imagined feasible in two manners: either by the animal moving its centre towards that point; or by the object being, through the joint instrumentality of the spines, and partly doubtless also of the water-feet, successively conveyed nearer to the centre, until it can be seized by the pedicellariae attached to the spines which proceed from the environs of the mouth (the bucal spines) whereupon it can be immediately taken into the bucal aperture, which is extensible as far as to these spines. It is probable that both these cases can occur, accordingly as the object is of greater or less bulk. As in all probability the movements of the animal, even when it is living in completely normal circumstances, are very sluggish and slow, and as the arms themselves cannot possibly act as instruments of prehension, it could scarcely be imagined possible that the animal without the help of these small organs would be able to provide itself with sufficient nourishment. But by this peculiar equipment, the animal is enabled in an extremely easy manner, to secure any prey that may be found within reach of the arms. It is indeed not rare to find in the captured specimens a whole fauna of various sorts of small animals (Annelides Crustaceans &c) hanging fast in different places to the arms, and often so firmly entangled between the spines as not to be extricable without much difficulty. Every little animal, which in its course along the bottom of the sea is so unfortunate as to come in too close contact with the slowly-gliding magnificent star, is immediately seized and retained by numerous microscopical forceps, and stopped in its career without being able by any exertions to liberate itself.

On the other hand this peculiarity in the Brisinga makes it comparatively easy to capture. No complicated tackle is required. Not even the ordinary simple dredge. It is quite sufficient to fasten to a heavy lead a thick rope's-end, the single strands of which are, as in the „swabs" used at sea, separated from each other, and only kept together at the part where the lead is attached. When such a swab is dragged slowly along the bottom, the loose strands spread themselves out like a fan over a considerable space, and sweep the bottom. If any part of the swab comes in contact with a creeping Brisinga, the latter will immediately become attached to it by the action of the pedicellaries, and entangled in the strands with its spiny arms, and can thus simply be drawn up, together with the swab, to the surface of the water. There is very seldom any risk that the animal should fall off. More frequently it will be found so well attached, that the greatest difficulty will be experienced in extricating the spiny arms uninjured from the threads. This very simple instrument was, as is well known, first systematically employed in the Porcupine's expedition under the name of „hempen tangles"; and has since been very extensively used in examining the bottom of the ocean.

2. The Vegetative Functions.

What I have to state of these functions is based less on direct observations of the living animal, than on the conclusions to which I have come by a more minute examination of the structure and relation of the organs herein concerned. Although there can generally here be no question of any thing else than what relates to the whole group of animals to which the Brisinga belongs, I feel bound for the sake of completeness to touch briefly on this part of the natural history of the Brisinga, especially as my conception of it is in several points rather different from that usually adopted.

A. Nutrition.

We have under this head briefly to notice: The reception of food, digestion, circulation of the blood, respiration and secretion, all which functions must on the whole be supposed to proceed exactly in the same manner as in all other star-fishes. As however there is much that in connexion with this subject is still very obscure; and as it is highly necessary to subject many points to renewed investigation, I think that it will not be out of place to develop here more particularly the views which I have been led to adopt by more minute examination of the present form.

a. Reception of food.

The food on which the Brisinga lives seems to consist of all sorts of smaller and larger deep-sea animals, annelides, crustaceans, rhizopodes &c. On the whole it does not seem to be dainty in its choice, but to utilise all the organic particles that come within its reach, and into its power. Even such animals as are provided with a firm calcareous crust, for instance shells and foraminifera are swallowed with equal avidity, and the organic particles of the same rapidly extracted. How, in all probability, the animal obtains its prey we have already considered. That the pedicellariae play an important part in such capture I think is indubitable. I consider it very probable that the animal does not only attack smaller organisms, but also animals or masses of organic matter which are too large to pass through the bucal aperture, even when it is extended to its greatest circumference. In this case the folds of the stomach are protruded more or less beyond the bucal aperture, and laid round the object or a part of it; so that the digestive cavity may in this case be said, in a manner, to lie outside of the body. It is by no means rare, especially in the other species Br. endecacnemos, to find specimens in which the folds of the stomach are in this manner protruded through the mouth, in a very remarkable degree, so as even to project far beyond the spines attached to the lower side of the disc, and thereby entirely to conceal the proper border of the mouth (see the delineation in Fauna littoralis Tab. IX, fig. 2).

b. The digestion.

From the walls of the stomach there is secreted, during the reception of the aliments, a fluid which seems to have a quickly dissolving and decomposing influence on the food; so that in a comparatively very short time the nourishing matter is extracted even from such organisms as, like shell-cased molluscs and foraminifera, are enveloped in a hard calcareous shell. The indigestible residuum of the aliments is, together with the extraneous parts, (the particles of mud) which enter the stomach at the same time, simply thrown out by the same way they came in. But the fluids, which can be more easily assimilated, are received into the upper stomachal cavity, whence they pass into the radial caeca, which will always be found filled with a greater or less quantity of oily juice (chylus). From the main trunks of the radial caeca this juice enters again into thin-skinned lateral recesses, in which probably the absorption or the transfer of the nourishing parts of this juice to the rest of the body, or conversion into blood, takes place. According to my conception, this is effected simply by a transudation through the walls of these lateral recesses, whereby the juice is thus immediately mixed with the fluid contained in the perivisceral cavity.

c. The circulation of the blood.

As is well known, Tiedemann supposed that he had found in the great Mediterranean star-fish Astropecten aurantiacus a completely developed blood-vessel system of veins and arteries, and assumes therefore in this case a completely developed circulation of the blood. The central organ of the circulation of the blood, or the heart, is considered by him to be the peculiar membranous organ which accompanies the stone canal, and which in his opinion connects itself with a dorsal and a ventral annular vessel whence the other blood vessels issue; the dorsal annular vessel with its ramifications representing the venous system, and the ventral annular vessel with the branches issuing from it, the arterial system. This complicated arrangement of the blood-vessel system described by him, which would also necessarily presuppose a complete circulation of the blood, has been, as it reasonably might be, considered referable to all star-fishes, without any one, so far as I know, having subsequently been able by direct investigation to demonstrate anatomically the existence of this system of vessels in other star-fishes, and thereby to confirm Tiedemann's statements. Neither have I, as already mentioned, been able to discover this system of vessels in the Brisinga. The only part which in this animal, as well as in other star-fishes, may easily be indicated is the so-called heart, the real nature and destination of which still appear to me to be highly problematical. Also in the Brisinga this organ (Tab. VI. fig. 6 h, fig. 8) accompanies the stone-canal, extending from the ventral to the dorsal side of the disc, where it terminates at a short distance from the stone-canal on the inner side of the madreporic body. The complicated system of veins, which according to Tiedemann's description is supposed to stand in connexion whith the heart I consider to be something quite different, namely simply ligaments serving to attach the stomach and the radial cæca to the dorsal skin. By repeated careful dissections I have succeeded in obtaining preparations of all these ligaments in their natural connexion with each other and with the adjacent parts (see Tab. VI. fig. 6) whereby a somewhat complicated structure is exhibited, in the chief features of which it is easy to recognise the arrangement indicated by Tiedemann for the supposed veins. I have however been able at the same time, to ascertain by satisfactory evidence the real nature of all these parts, differing widely from that of blood-vessels. As regards the supposed ventral, or so-called arterial blood-vessel system, my investigations in the Brisinga and other star-fishes have led me to the conclusion that we have only here to do with a system of narrow canal-like sinus, without any particular walls, covered immediately below by the chief parts of the nervous system, and not in any proper sense entitled to be called blood-vessels.

The blood is thus in the Brisinga, and as I have reason to believe also in other star-fishes, not inclosed in a special system of vessels, but freely suspended in the whole perivisceral cavity (cœloma) where it immediately surrounds and laves all the interior organs. That there should also be found in the perivisceral cavity a considerable quantity of water taken in from without, I do not regard as forming any objection to this opinion; on the contrary I hold such a mixture of blood to be quite necessary for its maintenance and purification; as special breathing apparatus is, at least in the Brisinga, entirely wanting. The locomotion of the blood-fluid contained in the perivisceral cavity is brought about by a lively ciliary movement of the whole interior surface of the skin, partly no doubt also by the contractions and expansions of the skin itself and of the central part of the digestive cavity or stomach. There can thus be no question here, properly speaking, of any real circulation of the blood in the usual signification of the expression; as the blood contained in the perivisceral cavity always surrounds immediately the organs enclosed in the same and thereby effects their alimentation.

There is however an important system of organs, the anomalous position of which in the star-fishes necessitates a peculiar arrangement of the blood-system; and that is the nervous system. While all the other vital organs have their place in the common perivisceral cavity (coeloma) the chief parts of the nervous system, the so-called ambulacral nerves, are, as already indicated, situated quite superficially immediately under the thin skin which lines the ventral furrows, and entirely separated from the perivisceral cavity by the interjacent ambulacral skeleton. In order that the nervous system might be alimented in the same manner as the other vital organs, it was therefore necessary that a part of the blood-fluid should be conducted to it. This is effected by means of the before mentioned system of canal-like sinus which is immediately bounded below by the central parts of the nervous system, and which has formerly, and doubtless erroneously, been regarded as composed of real blood-vessels of an arterial nature. How the blood-fluid from the perivisceral cavity is conducted into these canals, and whether the so-called heart really plays any part herein, is not yet so completely clear to me that I can venture to express any decided opinion. I have as above mentioned, not been able to indicate with certainty any direct communication between the upper end of the „heart" and the perivisceral cavity; and although its lower end seems to be in immediate contact with the circular sinus that lies inside of the buccal membrane, I have yet not succeeded in ascertaining by direct investigation that there is any actual communication in both cases. The question might probably be best decided by experimental injection in large living star-fishes, for which unfortunately I have no opportunity at present. That there really exists a communication between the said canals and the perivisceral cavity, I consider in any case as given; as the fluid contained in them corresponds entirely to that which is found in the perivisceral cavity, and like it contains small cell-like globules (blood cells) which are set in motion by an interior ciliary arrangement. Likewise I consider it to be very probable that at the point of the arms there exists a direct connexion between this latter and the canal-like blood-sinus which run along the ventral furrows.

d. The respiration.

No special organs of respiration are found in the Brisinga. I have sought in vain in the dorsal skin for the so-called respiratory tentacles which in most other star-fishes are so distinct and numerous. They are quite certainly wanting in the Brisinga. The respiration may therefore reasonably be supposed to stand in connexion with the reception of water into the interior of the body, which appears to take place continually. Of the parts of the water-system, the ampollæ belonging to the water-feet project more or less from the ambulacral pores into the perivisceral cavity, where they form along the upper side of the skeleton of the arm a double row from the base to the extreme point (see Tab. III, fig. 4 and 17). The extremely thin-skinned nature of these ampollæ in the Brisinga seems to make them well adapted for effecting a transmutation of gas between the water enclosed in them and the fluid of the perivisceral cavity. Moreover the direct reception of water which takes place in the perivisceral cavity itself, chiefly as we may suppose through the terminal section of the ambulacral vessels, must no doubt contribute in an essential degree to the purification and maintenance of the blood.

c. Secretion.

I have previously noticed as an apparatus of secretion, the peculiar and strongly developed glandular organ in the Brisinga, which is situated in the middle above the stomach between the latter and the dorsal skin, and from which there issues a short canal terminating on the dorsal side of the disc in a fine pore with a slightly excentric position. It is this pore which in the Brisinga, and indeed also in other star-fish, has been called the anal aperture, the narrow canal connected with it having been considered as a terminal section of the alimentary cavity or a real intestine. I have already remarked, in describing this apparatus, that in my opinion such a view is erroneous. Between the said canal and the cavity of the stomach, I have not been able to discover any direct connexion whatever; and even if any such connexion really existed, it would still be difficult to understand how this canal could act as a terminal intestine; for it is so extraordinarily narrow, that even the smallest solid particles could not possibly be expelled through it and through the likewise extremely fine dorsal pore. Neither have I ever seen real excrements expelled in this manner; all the indigestible remains of the aliments are on the contrary ejected again through the mouth. I can not therefore consider this canal in the Brisinga as any thing else than a simple issue for the glandular apparatus previously noticed; and I think it highly probable that many of the star-fishes which have been presumed to possess an anus, are really without it, but have only a similar small secretory pore.

The product of secretion is a colorless fluid developed in the organ which, according to its whole structure, is evidently glandulous. Concerning the nature of this secretion, it seems reasonable to regard it as a sort of urinary product, on which supposition the whole glandular apparatus would have to be considered as a blood-purifying organ similar to the kidneys in the higher animals. Such a function has also usually been previously ascribed in other star-fishes to the so-called interradial or rectal cæca, to which the organ in question evidently corresponds.

B. Propagation.

I am inclined to suppose that the Brisinga has two different means of propagation, a sexual and a non sexual process. Such an assumption will not preliminarily appear to be so entirely unreasonable; since we have (mainly through Lütken[1]) recently become acquainted with some Asteridæ in which, collaterally with the usual sexual propagation, we can distinctly demonstrate a multiplication by simple division. A non sexual propagation, somewhat different indeed from this, may I think be claimed for the Brisinga collaterally with the ordinary process.

a. The sexual propagation.

As in other star-fishes, only one sort of sexual organs, the ovaries, or the spermaries can be developed in the same individual. The sexes are therefore always separate. At the time when the propagation takes place, the ovaries, as well as the testes, swell very considerably; so that the dorsal skin of the arms comes into a state of extremely strong tension. The ripe sexual products issue from the sexual apertures, and are mixed together in the water without any actual copulation taking place. In the captured specimens the sexual products will often be observed issuing from the sexual apertures in the form of a more or less projecting plug, which only little by little is dissolved or becomes diffused in the water. The emission of the sexual products takes place thus as it seems very slowly; and the whole act of propagation extends therefore over a tolerably long period. Only when the specimens have attained their full size, have I found the sexual products mature. In younger specimens, we can indeed always discern both ovaries and testes, but they are still quite solid, with undeveloped contents. In the ovaries there are only found simple clear cells without any deposit of the opaque yellowish red yolk-mass peculiar to the mature ovum; and in the seminaries only the small elliptical bodies whence the characteristic filiform spermatozoa are subsequently developed. With regard to the time for propagation it appears chiefly to be limited to the summer months.

b. The non sexual propagation.

I have certainly not succeeded in ascertaining by direct observation the faculty in the Brisinga of such multiplication by non sexual means; and what I have to state on this subject will be for the present chiefly hypothetical. I feel however bound to produce the

[1] Beskrivelser af nogle nye eller mindre bekjendte Sjøstjerner, med nogle Bemærkninger om Selvdelingen hos Straaledyrene. (Oversigt over d. Kongl. Danske Vid. Selsk. Forhandl. 1872

reasons which have led me to adopt the notion that such a non sexual propagation does at times actually take place in the Brisinga.

There is one thing which must immediately be remarked by any one who has examined a sufficient number of specimens of this form; and that is the frequently very unequal development of the arms or rays. In nearly all the specimens examined by me one or more of the arms, and sometimes even most of them, proved to be in a more or less rudimentary state, and evidently only quite recently regenerated from the disc. That these newly formed arms had grown in the stead of fully developed arms which had been separated from the disc, was evident from the structure of the disc, and admits of no doubt. The question is now to explain in a reasonable manner the so frequent detachment of fully developed arms in the Brisinga. To assume that such detachment is caused by accidental external violence, or hostile attack of larger sea-animals, might certainly be admissible if the question was only of isolated cases. But where the occurrence proves to be so frequent, as my investigations have taught me, that it may even be considered as the general rule, while it is the exception to find specimens with all their arms equally developed; I should be more inclined to recognise a more normal phenomenon, namely a real voluntary act of the animal, a spontaneous detachment of one or more of its symmetrical principal parts (Antimera) that is to say a peculiar sort of division, the object of which is to effect a non sexual propagation. To state briefly my opinion, I think that every arm thus detached does not perish, but is destined to form a new individual by reproducing from its adoral extremity a new disc, which then, by a sort of budding, sends forth the other Antimera or arms belonging to a completely developed individual. I think I may be allowed to assume the possibility of such a propagation, when we consider the great self-substanciality of the arms of star-fishes generally, and especially of those of the Brisinga; and likewise that direct observations are not wanting which appear to prove that such regeneration may in isolated cases take place even in much more centralised star-fishes, for instance in the genus Asterias and Ophidiaster.

3. Faculty of regeneration and tenacity of life.

That the star-fishes possess an extraordinary power of regeneration is sufficiently well known. This is especially easy to ascertain in the forms that are found in the littoral belt, and therefore exposed to many external injuries, often bearing the marks of the most diversified damage, which yet does not appear to have any appreciable influence on the vital vigor of the animal. From the injured parts it may be observed that a very lively new formation takes place, whereby not only the wounded surfaces heal rapidly, but also the lost parts, with all the organs belonging to them, are in a shorter or a longer time completely regenerated. In the deep-sea star-fishes it is however much more rare to find traces of accidental mutilation, and that is by reason of the calm and quiet which always reign in the great depths of the sea, and which rarely exist in the litoral zone where so many sorts of external perturbations exercise their influence. It is however presumable that also the deep-sea star-fishes possess the same faculty and facility of repairing by regeneration all sorts of injuries. This appears very evidently, in the Brisinga. That lost arms can be completely reproduced again from the disc, has been already noticed; and likewise that we often find in the same specimens a great number of such small arms simultaneously sprouting forth. In the specimens delineated by Wyville Thomson (l. c.) there are represented no less than 5 such rudimentary arms in one uninterrupted series. Also in the middle of broken arms regeneration takes place in the same manner very easily. I have once observed such a case in the arm of a full grown male specimen where the reproduced part of the arm was evidently and sharply distinguished from the original basal piece. I shall have occasion in a subsequent section to notice a highly remarkable case, where one of the arms in an otherwise normally developed individual was bifurcate at the extremity (see Tab. II. fig. 3). This monstrous formation of the arm owes its origin without doubt to an accidental lesion and consequent regeneration. In this case the reproducing power shows even such a redundance that it has not confined itself to reproducing the lost piece only, but has done it doubly. It is, as already noticed, my conviction that even a single separated arm will be able to reproduce a completely new disc, with the other arms belonging to the same, as has already been stated with great probability with reference to the genus Ophidiaster and Linckia (see the above cited memoir of Mr. Lütken).

That the animal, in otherwise normal circumstances, possesses great tenacity of life under external injuries, is undoubted. It is a different question whether the animal would, under circumstances which may be regarded as exercising an injurious influence on all the vital functions, exhibit any unusual tenacity of life. Now the animal must undeniably find itself so situated when brought up from the deep, as is also clearly indicated by the convulsive agency whereby all the arms will almost always in this case detach themselves from their connexion with the disc. Nevertheless I have been able to keep such specimens divided into their separate parts, alive even for many days by supplying them with fresh sea-water in sufficiently large vessels.

I will mention one more apparently important fact in support of my hypothesis above set forth of the non sexual propagation, namely that the arms always shewed signs of life during a somewhat longer time than the disc itself whence they were detached. The chief seat of vital force seems thus to be rather in each single arm than in the disc itself, whence again it appears to be matter of inference that it would be more difficult for a disc detached from all its arms to reproduce a single arm, than for a single detached arm to form both the disc and all the other arms belonging to it.

VI

History of development.

(Ontogeny).

I must presume it very probable that the embryonic development of the Brisinga may exhibit peculiarities of very great interest, and perhaps will open for us a still clearer view of the nature of the Echinoderms in general; and I must so much the more regret that I can give no information as to this important point in the natural history of the Brisinga.

How the ova, when ejected from the ovaries, progress after fecundation; whether they produce, as seems to be the rule for star-fishes, a bilateral symmetrical freely swimming larva in which the first foundation of the future star-fish is found, or whether the development takes place more directly, as is the case with a much more limited number of them, must be decided by future investigation.

We may however by anticipation, and with some degree of confidence, assume the existence of the first named mode of development. My direct investigations as to the development do not begin until after that the animal has acquired the radiary form peculiar to the class.

1. Progressive development.

Under this head we have to treat of the changes in the appearance of the whole animal, and in the form and structure of the single parts which they undergo in the normal progressive growth, from the time when the animal has acquired its radiary form, until it attains the fully developed state. These changes are in general such as are common to all individuals without exception, and must be well distinguished from the changes in particular details which usually occur later, partly determined by purely, accidental causes partly in consequence of a more or less abnormal development.

a. Early Stage of the Brisinga.

From the same locality whence I obtained my supply of Brisingas, I once chanced to get out of the mud brought up in the dredge a little tiny 10-armed young star-fish which, in spite of its very different appearance at first sight, may nevertheless with full certainty be classed as a Brisinga in a very early stage of development, exhibiting in more than one respect points of very special interest.

The specimen (Tab. IV, fig. 38, 39) has only a disc-diameter of 2.50 Mm., and has all its arms 10 in number in natural connexion with the disc. The length of the arms cannot accurately be ascertained; as in all of them the extreme point is broken off. They do not however appear to have exceeded in length the double diameter of the disc. Now what immediately appears remarkable in them is that they proceed from the disc apparently quite in the ordinary manner like simple prolongations or expansions of it, without any indication on the exterior of any sharp limitation as in the adult Brisinga. Altogether this young animal is in its whole habitus a completely normal star-fish resembling most the young Solaster papposus; and it would not easily have occurred to me that the little animal was a real Brisinga if I had not noticed in it a peculiarity which induced me to examine it more minutely. Quite unlike the young Solaster, it remained clinging with great tenacity to every object it come in contact with, exactly in the same manner as a Pedicellaster, which already would at once indicate a very special development of its pedicellariæ. On examining the latter microscopically, I found to my surprise that they corresponded even in the minutest details to those of the adult Brisinga, and, as in the latter, a great many of them were crowded together on the skin-sheaths of the arm-spines. A further examination of the specimen brought to light many other characteristics, demonstrating with absolute certainty that we have here really a young Brisinga before us.

Let us therefore consider this young animal somewhat more closely. Viewed from above (fig. 39) it exhibits, as before mentioned, all the characteristics of a completely normal young star-fish. In the dorsal skin there appear already to be formed various calcareous deposits. In the interior there may be remarked an extremely fine hyaline calcareous net, perforated with regular holes, and here, strangely enough, forming large connected divisions of irregular form. Each of these divisons consists however only of the most primitive calcareous elements widely different from the complicated calcareous net which is found in developed star-fishes. From these calcareous nets in the skin there issue at regular intervals larger and smaller spines, a couple of which were of quite unusual length and extremely thin, almost like bristles, but every one enveloped in its separate cuticular sheath. In the angle between two contiguous arms there may be observed a more regularly formed plate, which without doubt is the rudiment of the wedge-plate found here in fully developed specimens. But no distinct trace is yet to be seen of the marginal plates that stand in connexion with the wedge-plate. Neither can there be certainty distinguished any evident madreporic body. The arms issue like immediate prolongations from and round the disc; they are broadest at the base, and thence rapidly and evenly tapering towards the extremity which however as before mentioned was broken off in them all. Through the transparent dorsal skin of the arms, in which every trace of calcareous keels or transverse ridges is still wanting, there appears the subjacent ambulacral skeleton with its medial elevated crest formed by the dorsal part of the ambulacral plates. The single vertebræ are of a particularly narrow and elongated form. Along each side of the arms there is seen a single row of spines, which are all provided with a distinct skin-sheath thickly larded with pedicellaries. According to their position, they appear to answer to the outer furrow-spines in the developed individuals.

If we turn the specimen round, and view it from the ventral side (see fig. 40) the naked skin-like area which occupies nearly the whole of the underside of the disc, with the widely gaping circular oral aperture (o) in the middle of it, strikes the eye immediately. Only in the extreme periphery there appear those calcareous parts which support the disc and the arms (the ambulacral skeleton) which as regards the disc forms an extremely narrow frame, composed of a single set of vertebræ, whence the skeleton of the arms takes its issue. In conformity herewith we see only a single circle of 20 water-feet belonging to the disc. These water-feet are placed in pairs at the extremities of the ambulacral furrows which run along the ventral side of the arms; each pair separated from the next by an obtusely conical calcareous piece (ad⁵) projecting inwards from the angle between 2 arms, and formed by the 2 contiguous adambulacral plates belonging to the 2 adjacent vertebræ. The ventral furrows of the arms taper rapidly outwards, and are, between each successive pair of water-feet, distinctly instricted. The adambulacral plates which limit the ventral furrows on the sides are long and narrow, yet still indistinctly separated from each other, and only furnished each with a single spine in the middle. Likewise each of the innermost adambulacral plates (ad⁵) belonging to the disc and joined together in one piece, is furnished in the middle with a long spine directed obliquely downwards and outwards. Of the oral spines, spread out fan-like towards the mouth, which in fully developed specimens are so distinct, there is yet no trace to be seen. Immediately before the interior extremity of the ambulacral furrows, and partly covered by the point of the 2 contiguous innermost adambulacral plates, there extends round the whole ventral side of the disc a narrow calcareous ring, to which the oral membrane (m) is attached. It answers to the circular ridge projecting inwards from the oral ring in adult animals, and consists similarly of 20 single pieces, which, immediately before the ambulacral furrows and the point of the interradial spaces, are connected with each other by evident sutures.

It will be seen from the above description that the disc in the young Brisinga mentioned, although externally appearing to be rather large in proportion to the arms, is yet really, with due regard to the skeleton, still more reduced than in the full grown animal;

as only one single set of vertebræ enters into the composition of the disc; while the following set, which in the adult animal always continues in firm connexion with the oral ring, does here evidently not belong to the ring but to the arms. As regards this innermost set of vertebræ, their form and structure appear here to correspond so perfectly with the proper vertebræ of the arms, that we may really also consider them as belonging to the arms. In this manner there will thus remain only the narrow calcareous ring to which the oral membrane is attached, that can be considered as a special skeleton-formation belonging to the disc; while all the remaining skeleton is only formed by the 10 arms, which are so arranged around a common centre that their interior vertebræ are contiguous and grow together with each other. The important inferences which may be hence deduced for a correct appreciation of the nature of the star-fishes, will be noticed more particularly in a subsequent section.

b. Development of the disc.

The structure of the disc has been already above noticed in a very early stage of development, whereby it appears evidently enough that the exterior set of vertebræ, which in fully developed specimens enters into the composition of the calcareous ring, does not originally belong to the disc, but represents the interior vertebræ of the arms. In the beginning there is also between both these sets of vertebræ, a movable muscular connexion similar to that between the other vertebræ of the arms; so that it is in fact only the interior set of vertebræ which serves as support for the disc itself. During the subsequent growth and enormous development of the arms, it becomes however necessary that the skeleton of the disc should acquire a greater solidity than could be produced by only a single set of vertebræ; for which cause the interior vertebræ of the arms have to give up their mobility little by little, and, by connecting themselves with the original calcareous ring, to contribute to its more powerful development.

In quite young specimens with a diameter of disc of 10—12ᵐᵐ and a length of arms of 60—70ᵐᵐ these vertebræ still retain in some degree their original self-substantiality. They are (see Tab. V, fig. 13 & 15) comparatively to the yet slightly developed interior vertebræ, considerably more prominent, and even project distinctly beyond the periphery of the calcareous ring, being bounded on each side by a rather deep sinus in the calcareous ring, which indicates the place, where the wedge-plate rises. The connexion with the interior set of vertebræ has however already acquired so much firmness that these vertebræ, as in adult specimens, always remain attached to the disc when the arms are separated from it.

With respect to the exterior form of the disc in such young specimens (the smallest having only a disc-diameter of 10ᵐᵐ) it differs from that of the full grown, in the more or less evidently projecting radial parts, as well as in its considerably greater flatness or thinness, and in its generally weaker and less compact appearance. It is like the arms, of a

8

very pale reddish color, and when held up against the light so transparent that several of the interior organs may be distinctly seen through the dorsal skin.

The dorsal spines are proportionally smaller and more dispersed; and only a few of those attached nearer to the centre may sometimes be distinguished by a peculiar strongly elongated bristle-like form, evidently a relict from the embryonic state; the madreporic body occupies the same characteristic place as in the adult specimens, but is always very small and only slightly convex. The spines attached on the lower side of the disc (to the adambulacral plates) are relatively much shorter than in full grown specimens, and fewer in number; and of the oral spines directed towards the mouth, there are only 2 or 4 developed for each interradial space.

c. Development of the arms.

In the little juvenile Brisinga previously mentioned, the extreme points of all the arms were, as already stated, broken off; so that their exact form and length could not be accurately ascertained. I have noticed as characteristic the less distinct demarcation between them and the disc; the entire absence of calcareous ribs and transverse ridges, and the presence of only a single row of spines on each side (the exterior furrow-spines).

We have however even in fully developed specimens of the Brisinga the best opportunity for studying the development of the arms, and for tracing their changes to a yet much earlier stage of development than in the young one mentioned. There is always taking place in the Brisinga, as before stated, a continually repeated reproduction of new arms, in place of those previously detached from the disc. But it is here to be remarked that these arms, formed by a sort of germination, develope themselves apparently in a manner somewhat different from that in which the arms originally belonging to the young animals are developed.

In the earliest stage of development these new arms sprouting from the disc (see Tab. VI, fig. 18) have only the appearance of inconsiderable conical processes, issuing nearer to the ventral side from the middle of the radial spaces. But on closer examination the rudiments of the most important parts may already be distinguished. The extremity always exhibits a distinct button-like enlargement, from the lower side of which there projects in a horisontal direction a relatively large cylindrical appendage (b) which is the previously mentioned peculiar terminal apparatus, the first evidently developed organ that appears. On the upper side, and especially on the terminal enlargement of the arms, there appear (see fig. 11, 12, 13) already several pedicellariæ developing themselves, but still quite in a cellular form, and distributed without any distinct order over the skin. Below there may be seen very distinctly the rudiments of a limited number (12–14) water-feet (w) in the form of small button-like warts arranged in 2 longitudinal rows, and rapidly increasing in size towards the base of the arm, with a distinctly marked raised line (n) running between

the two rows, which line is the ambulacral nerve that forms a well defined club-shaped
enlargement (b) at the base of the organ of sense (a). Of spines no trace is yet to be
seen. Only after that the nascent arm has increased somewhat more in length, there may
be observed on each side of the water-feet a single row of regularly arranged sinuosities in
the skin, wherein the calcareous particles begin to develop themselves (fig. 13 p). These
are the growing furrow-spines. Nearer to the dorsal side there may be seen a similar row
of bag-like enlargements in the skin, inclosing calcareous particles in a state of progressive
development, but more irregularly arranged. They represent the growing marginal spines,
and on those situated nearest to the base a few pedicellariæ have already begun to develop
themselves (see fig. 15 p). The pedicellariæ which appear in the dorsal skin have in the
mean-time developed themselves further, and now begin to be arranged in distinct raised
transverse stripes or bands. The rudiments of water-feet have increased considerably in
number; and those placed nearest the base have already acquired a cylindrical form and
commenced their activity (fig. 15 w). The terminal organ of sense has during the progress
of this development retained approximately its original form and size, but is now partially
overhung by a distinct protecting calcareous plate with accompanying spines and pedicellariæ (see fig. 14 & 15).

The further development of the arms consists now essentially in a successive increase of joints or metamera proceeding from the base of the terminal enlargement, with a
corresponding increase in the number of water-feet and spines; while the arm grows rapidly
in length (see Tab. I, fig. 4, 5, 6 e, Tab. II, fig. 1 & 2).

The transverse bands over the dorsal skin, which are covered with pedicellariæ,
appear now both in greater number and with greater distinctness and regularity; and the
marginal spines are more and more elongated, especially at the base. Even after that the
arm has attained a length of 30—40ᵐᵐ there is still no trace to be seen externally of the
spined calcareous ribs so characteristic of the full grown animal. Only in a much later stage
namely after that the organs of generation have begun to develop themselves, these ribs
begin to appear as quite narrow slightly raised calcareous stripes, on which the spines are
still only short and indistinct (see Tab. I, fig. 1). The marginal spines have already long
ago attained their full development, as also the exterior furrow spines; but the interior
furrow spines do not begin to develop themselves until much later; nay, it appears that
even after the animal has attained its full development, a constant increase takes place in
the number of these small spines ranged nearest to the ventral furrow. The arm which in
the beginning was thickest at the base and thence rapidly tapering towards the end, begins
now to be somewhat instricted at the base and thereby to be more sharply distinguished
from the disc; as the dorsal skin lies here close on the subjacent ambulacral skeleton;
while at some distance from the base, this skin begins to be more and more elevated above
it and stretched to the sides. The characteristic almost fusiform appearance, which the
basal part of the arm often exhibits in adult specimens (see Tab. I, fig. 12, Tab. II, fig. 1)

8*

is due to the strongly developed organs of generation lying within it. If these organs, as is the case in other seasons than in the summer, are less developed, then neither will the arms in full grown specimens exhibit such a remarkable enlargement; although they are always at the base considerably thinner than they are further out from it.

d. Development of the ambulacral skeleton.

To examine the development of the ambulacral skeleton, it is only necessary to isolate from the disc a recently formed arm-shoot, and to put it in a solution of potass, which will quickly make all the organic parts transparent. On examining the arm-shoot under the microscope with sufficient magnifying power (see Tab. VI, fig. 13, 14. 15) the calcareous particles which are to form the ambulacral skeleton will then be distinctly seen developing themselves in the interior. As the formation of the various joints or metamera, of which the arm is composed, always proceeds from the base of the terminal knob-like enlargement of the arm, the youngest or earliest foundations of the vertebræ will always be found nearest to the same, and the nearer to the base of the arms the more developed they will be found. Thus in one and the same preparation, we have a whole series of successive stages of development before us. Every vertebra is formed of numerous reticular ramified hyaline calcareous staves, which take their issue from 4 different points or centres answering to the single calcareous plates of which each vertebra is originally composed. These points of ossification of the vertebræ are situated somewhat nearer to the ventral than to the dorsal side of the arm, and they are arranged in pairs slightly varying in height, and regularly alternating with each other. The pair situated nearest to the medial line, and in a more dorsal position (fig. 14 a), forms the foundation for the ambulacral plates; that more remote from the middle, and nearer the ventral side (ad), represents the adambulacral plates. The former pair appears first, and afterwards successively the other. Originally these points of ossification lie widely separated from each other, and only during the further development and ramification of the calcareous particles approach each other little by little, so as at last to become united partly by suture, partly by muscular ligaments.

The manner in which the ramification of these calcareous parts composing the vertebræ proceeds, may be traced very distinctly in a recently formed arm-shoot. First of all there appears only a little angular calcareous granule (fig. 17, 18) which then shoots out a certain number (usually 6) radiating processes (fig. 19) situated in the same plane. Each of these processes divides itself then at the extremity, or shoots out in 2 diverging branches (fig. 20) which are again subdivided, and at last partially coalesce with those adjacent, and thereby, together with the original processes, form the boundaries of a single ring of oblong apertures (fig. 21). By a dichotomic subdivision of the outermost processes continued in the same manner, there is little by little formed a thin calcareous disc (fig. 22) perforated with numerous holes ranged with tolerable regularity in concentric order. This disc begins likewise subsequently to increase in thickness; as processes issue also from the surfaces of the disc, ramifying themselves in a similar manner. At last the ramification of the calcareous staves becomes so manifold and dense, that the whole forms a compact calcareous mass, in which however the original reticular or lattice-work formation may easily be observed by applying sufficient magnifying power (fig. 23, 24).

The ambulacral plates, which thus originally, like the adambulacral plates, had the form of thin circular discs, increase relatively very rapidly in volume, and soon acquire (see fig. 14, a) a transverse position on each side of the medial line. Both ends, the exterior as well as the interior, become gradually enlarged, and meet the nearest adjacent ambulacral plates belonging to the same side, whereby these plates acquire a somewhat fusiform shape. Between them there will thus remain oval apertures, which are the ambulacral pores, whence the water-feet project. The interior extremity of the ambulacral plates developes itself then more strongly than the exterior, and begins to raise itself up in the interior of the arm to form the dorsal ridge of the arm-vertebræ which is afterwards so prominent. Still however the ambulacral plates of each pair are separated in the medial line by a distinct fissure widened between the vertebræ (see fig. 16, a). The adambulacral plates (ad) grow relatively much more slowly, and remain therefore in respect of size far behind the nearest ambulacral plates: they are a little elongated, and ranged in a somewhat oblique direction in the intervals between the exterior ends of the ambulacral plates, and soon come in contact with these extremities.

The further development of the skeleton of the arm consists in each pair of ambulacral plates belonging to a vertebra growing together with each other and with the respective adambulacral plates. Afterwards the whole vertebra becomes gradually elongated during the further growth of the arm (fig. 16). In the young Brisinga above described even the interior vertebræ of the arm were as long as they were broad; and in young specimens with a disc-diameter of 10ᵐᵐ the joints of the arm (see Tab. V, fig. 15) are still quite unusually elongated in comparison with those of full grown individuals, in which, in the whole basal section, they are scarcely half as long as they are broad. As to the ambulacral skeleton of the disc, it has been already stated that it consists originally (in the earliest stages of development) only of the interior arm-joints that are connected with each other round a common centre (see Tab. V, fig. 11, 12). Besides the ambulacral and adambulacral plates belonging to these vertebræ, there are still only the so-called parietal plates (p) distinctly developed; these are however yet very small, and appear indeed only to contribute to the formation of the circular border (x) to which the oral membrane is attached. Of the wedge-plate only slight indications are observable (w), and these seem to shew that they ought rather to be reckoned among the calcareous parts of the cuticular system than as belonging to the ambulacral skeleton; although they are subsequently firmly connected with the latter. The same may be said with even greater certainty of the dorsal marginal plates, which are connected with the wedge-plate and which in like manner are, in fully developed specimens, firmly connected with the oral ring. but in the early stage appear only in the form of 2 thin bone pegs (r) loosely attached to the oral ring. Of the 2 following pairs of marginal plates belonging to the arms there is still, in the young animal above described, not the smallest trace to be seen.

In specimens with a disc-diameter of 11—12ᵐᵐ the oral ring (fig. 15) is still only very slightly developed; although it already consists of all the calcareous pieces which, in fully developed individuals, enter into its composition. It is especially very thin and flat: so that its upper surface is nearly horizontal, and lies about level with the skeleton of the arm; while in full grown individuals it is strongly convex, and towards the interior considerably raised above the skeleton of the arm. This comes mainly from the slight development of the interior set of vertebræ, which still retain much of their original appearance similar to that of the arm-vertebræ. It has been before mentioned that the exterior set of vertebræ, which likewise belong to the oral ring, and which in full grown individuals are considerably reduced in size, correspond in the early stage completely with the arm-vertebræ both in size and form, as well as by their looser connexion with the interior set of vertebræ, being moreover distinctly salient in the periphery of the oral ring. In consequence of the peculiar form of the oral ring hereby produced, the wedge-plates (fig. 14, 15 w), which in full grown specimens are more or less vertical, lie here in almost perfectly horizontal position; and on each side of them there appear, on the upper surface, the 2 pairs of ambulacral pores clearly and distinctly limited, the one behind the other.

c. Development of the cuticular skeleton.

The development of the calcareous particles enclosed in the dorsal skin proceeds exactly in the same manner as the development of the ambulacral skeleton, by a radiary ramification of originally simple isolated calcareous granules. In the dorsal cuticle of the disc, this development of the calcareous pieces to which the disc-spines are attached, is easily observed in quite young specimens, in which these calcareous pieces have still partially the form of small thin perforated circular discs. In the young specimen above described there is in the dorsal cuticle a more continuous extraordinarily thin calcareous net with wide circular meshes (Tab. VI. fig. 33), evidently a relict from the embryonic state, and which is afterwards replaced by the usual limited calcareous parts corresponding with the spines. Just opposite to the angles between the bases of the arms there can however be discerned 10 somewhat more distinctly limited plates, but of the same fine reticular structure. These plates (see Tab. IV. fig. 39) belong here most undoubtedly to the skin, but enter subsequently into connexion with the rudimentary wedge-plates, and form the tubercular prominence afterwards so conspicuous on the same.

The dorsal transverse ribs are indeed not outwardly visible until after that the arm has already attained a considerable development; but their foundation is laid very early,

63

and simultaneously with the formation of the ambulacral skeleton. Even in the very earliest foundations of the arms (see Tab. VI, fig. 15) there may be observed in the dorsal cuticle, immediately behind the terminal enlargement, 3 longitudinal rows of calcareous particles (r) forming themselves in the same manner as the ambulacral and adambulacral plates. These appear in the beginning (next to the terminal enlargement of the arms) quite separate, in the form of the usual regularly perforated circular discs; but in the subsequent progressive ramification of the calcareous staves connecting them, the 3 calcareous plates lying in a transverse row approach each other little by little until they coalesce, and thus in connexion form continuous transverse bands. At each end of these transverse bands there is developed already at a very early stage, a spine (p) which is the marginal spine. In the beginning, such calcareous particles in the dorsal skin develop themselves constantly from the basis of the terminal enlargement. There are thus formed more and more of the calcareous transverse bands. But after that the arm has attained a certain length this formation ceases. The arm continues however to grow by a constantly continued formation of new joints, which gradually force the first formed joints nearer to the base of the arm. Hence it is easily explained that these calcareous particles, which afterwards form the transversal spined cross-ribs, although they originally proceeded from the extremity of the arm, at last become far removed from it and confined only to the basal section.

It appears that besides the above-noticed calcareous particles specially imbedded in the skin, there are also a number of calcareous plates which belong to the cuticular skeleton, and which subsequently enter into intimate connexion with the ambulacral skeleton, namely the wedge-plates and dorsal marginal plates standing in connexion with the skeleton of the disc, also the 2 pairs of marginal plates which are found at the base of the arms, and finally the calcareous plate which covers the terminal organ of sense. This last (fig. 13—15, p l) is formed already very early, simultaneously with the ambulacral skeleton, as a net of thin calcareous staves ranged in a half-circle, whence subsequently thin spines take their issue (fig. 25). The dorsal marginal plates of the arms appear on the contrary not to form themselves until considerably later (see fig. 16, r, r).

f. Development of the spines.

The first spines which appear distinctly on the arms are, as before mentioned, the exterior furrow spines. They form (see fig. 13, p) first, close to each side of the ambulacral skeleton, a regular row of short cylindrical cuticular processes, each answering to a separate adambulacral plate. In the interior of these processes there appears first a little angular calcareous granule (fig. 26), which then, in the usual manner, begins to shoot out radiating processes whereby there is formed a simple perforated disc (fig. 27). From the middle of one surface of this disc, there arise a certain number of thin calcareous staves, close together, which rapidly grow in length (fig. 28). After these calcareous staves have attained a certain size, they shoot out, at right angles and at regular intervals, short lateral processes which grow together with the nearest calcareous staves (fig. 29, 30). Accordingly as the original number of staves may have been greater or smaller, there is at last formed a more or less complicated latticed process which is the proper calcareous spine; while the basal disc forms the enlarged joint-surface whereby the spine is subsequently articulated with the adambulacral plates. When the spine has attained a certain size, there begin to appear, at the end of the cuticular sheath, some few cell-like bodies projecting more or less from the same, and having small calcareous granules contained in them (fig. 31); this is the first development of the pedicellariae. All the other spines are formed precisely in the same manner. The marginal spines on the growing arms and the spines situated on the terminal enlargement of the arm appear nearly at the same time. The last named (fig. 32) are usually remarkable for their particularly slender shape, and for being originally formed of 2 or 3 strongly elongated calcareous staves connected with each other at regular intervals by horisontal intermediary bars. Of the spines belonging to the calcareous ribs of the arms, no trace is to be observed before the arm has attained a considerable development. They shew themselves then first as insignificant processes which however grow rapidly, and in adult specimens exhibit the circlets of spines, repeated at certain intervals around the dorsal side of the basal section of the arm, so specially characteristic of this species.

Among the spines situated on the dorsal side of the disc, we may sometimes observe in very young specimens a spine here and there of a quite unusual form strongly elongated and slender almost like a bristle. In the little young animal above described all the spines seem to have been of this nature; but most of them were already, when the animal was captured, more or less injured and some quite broken off. I succeeded however with some certainty in getting an idea of their original appearance. They are, as has been said, very strongly elongated and slender, quite hyaline and finely latticed like the ordinary spines, but very distinguishable by not being smooth, shewing several consecutive distinctly enlarged sections, each of which shoots out in a certain number of sharp points (fig. 34). The whole spine is hereby distinctly echinulated at regular intervals from the very base; while on the ordinary spines only the extreme end exhibits some few microscopic points. These peculiar spines belong, as it appears, only to the embryonic state; they afterwards disappear entirely, and are replaced by the usual spines which form themselves in the same manner as the arm-spines.

g. Development of the pedicellariae.

On the dorsal side of the very earliest foundations of the arms, as also on the cuticular sheaths of the spines which afterwards grow out of the arms, there appear, as has already been noticed, a greater or less number of these peculiar small organs, but mostly very far from being developed or in activity. We have thus here occasion to study the first formation and further successive development of these organs. It is however by no means necessary to depend only on such growing arms for opportunity of studying the development of the pedicellariæ. This investigation may be executed quite as well, and much more easily, on any developed arm; as, throughout the whole life of the animal, there seems to be a continual new formation of these organs, especially on the cuticular sheaths of the spines of the arms.

On examining more closely the cuticular sheath of one of the long spines of the arm, it will be found that the pedicellariæ in this exterior part are all fully developed and of the structure above described; while those nearer the base become gradually more rudimentary, until at last one can only observe a layer of simple cells surrounding the root of the spine (see fig. 31). This simple stratum of cells is the starting point for the progressive development of the pedicellariæ from the base. In the interior of the cells the development of the 3 calcareous particles above described can be very distinctly traced. They appear first (fig. 32) as 3 small widely separate granules situated in one row, and all nearly of the same size. Then the 2 outside granules which represent the side-pieces develope themselves more rapidly than the middle-piece, and soon assume a distinct triangular form (fig. 33) while the middle-piece still appears only like a little indistinctly angular granule. 2 of the 3 corners of the side-pieces now increase (see fig. 34) rapidly in length, developing themselves each in its manner; so that it can soon be discerned which of them is to form the proper forceps, and which shall become the lower plate-shaped process; but the 3d corner is relatively less developed, and only increases a little in breadth so as to form the vertical dentated edge projecting inwards from the middle of the side-pieces. The middle-piece now begins also to develope itself, by the extrusion in different directions of 4 cylindrical processes, 2 longer and 2 shorter, whereby it acquires, when viewed from above, the form of an irregular cross. In the subsequent development (see fig. 35) the 2 processes issuing from the side-pieces increase more and more in length, bending inwards towards the medial line. They are however quite simple, without teeth or plate-like enlargements; the upper one truncated at the extremity; the lower, conically pointed. The upper process, or the proper forceps, soon begins however (see fig. 36) to assume its characteristic spade-like form; and from each side of the truncated extremity, there protrudes a sharp corner, forming the exterior tooth of those which subsequently appear. The middle-piece now changes its form rapidly; small processes beginning to grow from the lower side, and again connecting themselves by their extremities, forming thereby the commencement of the perforated plates which subsequently appear, and which serve for the insertion of the motor muscles of the side-pieces. In the same manner the hitherto simply conical processes of the 2 side-pieces afterwards begin also little by little (see fig. 37) to assume their definitive plate-like form; as small processes issue from their exterior sides, and finally connect themselves by the extremities, so as to circumclude the characteristic oval apertures, in the periphery of which

9

the before mentioned muscles are attached. All 3 pieces come while undergoing this change closer together; and the articulation between the side-pieces and the middle-piece is effected in the manner which characterises the developed pedicellariæ. The changes described affect only the calcareous particles which develop themselves in the interior of the pedicellariæ, and which therefore are to be considered as a secretive product of the plasma of the original cell. The soft surrounding parts, or the cuticular sheath, are formed immediately by a simple readaptation of the whole cell. Already in a very early stage of development, there may be observed (see fig. 34), on the exterior side of the cell, a slight insinuosity like an incipient division. This insinuosity becomes little by little deeper and deeper, and represents at last a deep incision dividing the cell, into 2 broad lobes, each of which includes the anterior extremity of one of the side-pieces. These lobes unite themselves, during the further development, directly with the 2 movable flaps of the pedicellaria. At the same time the whole cell, formerly sunk in the skin, rises little by little above the surface, so as at least only to remain attached to it by a thin continuation, which becomes the flexible stem whereby the pedicellaria is fastened to the skin. When this stem is fully formed, then all the other parts belonging to the pedicellaria have also attained their definitive development; and it now begins to participate in the common function of all these small organs, to seize and hold fast all objects that come in connexion with them.

B. Divergent development.

The phenomena of development noticed in the preceeding lines are such as are common to all individuals, and generally do not only apply to the whole genus Brisinga, but partly also to all the other star-fishes. We come now to a series of changes which usually do not take place until the animal has attained a much more advanced age, and which go in a more divergent direction. These changes manifest themselves as more or less distinctly marked differences in the external form of the body, and in the particular details, between the different individuals. We have again to distinguish the more ordinary deviations from those dependent on quite accidental causes, and therefore to be regarded as more abnormal deviations.

a. Individual variations

On examining a series of individuals, it will soon be found that the individual variations in the present species range within tolerably wide limits. The variations apply partly to the number of the arms or ambulacra, partly to the form and arrangement of the different appendages belonging to the skin, and partly to the color.

Firstly as regards the ambulacra, the present species is in this respect distinguished in a remarkable degree from the other species of Brisinga. While in this latter the number of arms in all the specimens hitherto examined, has been always without exception 11, answering to the specific denomination „endecacnemos". I have found in the specimens of the present species examined by me a remarkable inconstancy in this respect; so that it is very difficult to say what number should be regarded as the normal number.

Of the 22 more or less perfect specimens examined by me, 7 were 9-armed; 9, 10-armed; 5, 11-armed, and 1, 12-armed: hence it appears that 9-armed, 10-armed and 11-armed specimens are about equally numerous; while it seems that specimens with more than 11 arms are very rare: since out of 22 specimens, only one was found with 12 arms. I do not however consider it improbable that, on examination of a greater number, it may be found that the inconstancy in the number of antimera ranges within still wider limits; and that specimens may be found with fewer than 9 and more than 12 arms. The specimen delineated by W. Thomson (l. c.) has thus, according to the drawing, no less than 13 arms. If this is really correct, then the number of arms in the present species would vary at least from 9 to 13: a very remarkable inconstancy in an animal of radiate construction. This variation in the number of antimera or ambulacra, does not however appear to be the result, as might be supposed, of a subsequent divergent development. On the contrary, I have reason to presume that the number of arms in each individual is already fixed in the embryo or larva body of the star-fishes, and continues unchanged during the whole life of the animal; for I have never seen on the disc the smallest sign of any new formation of ambulacra. All were, independently of the greater or smaller development of the arms, exactly of the same appearance and uniform development. Neither are the younger individuals distinguished by having fewer arms than the older ones. The little tiny young Brisinga above described had 10 arms distinctly developed, just as in most adult specimens; and of the 3 young individuals with a disc-diameter of 10 – 12mm, which I have had occasion to examine, only one was 9-armed, while the other two were 10-armed.

As regards the length of the arms in proportion to the diameter of the disc, it is far from being constantly the same in all individuals; nay even in one and the same individual, we may often find a considerable difference in the length of the arms, which in great part is caused by the regeneration of new arms taking place at various times, in stead of the older arms previously detached from the disc.

With respect to the number and arrangement of the calcareous transverse ribs on the basal part of the arm, we find an infinity of variations; and even in one and the same individual there will often be some difference on the different arms. The number in adult specimens seems to vary at least from 9 to 11. The number of the soft transverse bands covered with pedicellariæ and arranged in the intervals between these calcareous ribs, is likewise very variable. Sometimes there is only one (see Tab. II, fig. 2) sometimes — and

9

this seems to be the most usual case — 3 (fig. 1); more rarely the number is greater, up to 7; but in this case the transverse bands are usually interrupted in several places, and rudimentary (fig. 6). In like manner the spines attached along the calcareous ribs are very differently developed. Sometimes they are proportionally small, and in great numbers (fig. 4) sometimes the number is more limited, in which case they usually — especially towards the sides — attain a very considerable length (almost like the exterior furrow-spines).

Also the disc itself is subject to several variations. Its form is seldom perfectly circular, but often broader on one side, and irregular in a greater or less degree. Its dorsal spines are likewise in different individuals more or less developed, sometimes higher and more closely packed, sometimes lower and more spread. Finally the form and size of the madreporic body is subject to divers variations, even in equally developed individuals. It is however always naked, and never, as in the other species endecacnemos, covered with spines. The color of the animal varies, as already stated, through a series of tints, from light orange to deep purple red.

b. Accidental variations.
(Monstrosities).

Under this head I would class 2 cases which I have observed, and in which one of the arms in an otherwise normally and fully developed individual exhibited an appearance very different from what is usual.

Both cases were evidently caused by accidental mutilation, and consequent regeneration of the arm. In one instance the arm was very short, scarcely half as long as the others, but nevertheless in its basal section quite as much developed as the others, with swelling organs of generation, and well developed calcareous ribs and spines; while the exterior part of the arm was very slightly developed, and sharply distinguished from the rest of the arm, being in the form of a little thin lash-like appendage with rudimentary spines and water-feet. The arm had evidently been quite lately broken off at this place; and from the wounded surface, there had sprouted a nascent new arm to replace the lost part. I have also observed a perfectly similar instance in the Brisinga endecacnemos (see Tab. VII, fig. 1 a).

In the second case the arm was of the usual length, but highly remarkable for having the extremity bifurcate, or going out in 2 nearly equally long branches completely normally formed with all appertaining parts, and having at each end the terminal organ of sense (Tab. II, fig. 3). The ambulacral furrow running along the arm divided itself, at the issue of these two branches, precisely in the same manner as in a Pentacrinus or an Antedon; and the ambulacral skeleton seemed likewise to have been similarly affected. That an accidental mutilation of the arm had also in this case been the disturbing cause, is undoubted; but, instead of the single regeneration of the lost part, the reproduction has taken place in a double form; so that from the wounded surface there have sprouted forth 2 separate nascent arms, which have been further developed each for itself. Monstrosities analogous to these have already been observed in some exotic star-fishes, the Oreaster gigas and Astropecten aurantiacus.

VII.

Distribution and occurrence.

(Chorology).

With regard to the distribution and occurrence of the present species, much valuable information has been obtained by the great English expeditions, that may in connexion with my own observations, help us to form tolerably accurate notions on this subject. It appears to be everywhere a true deep-sea form, and, like most deep-sea animals, to have a very wide geographical distribution.

a. Horisontal distribution.

As already noticed, I have hitherto found the present species of Brisinga, on our coast, only on the fishing ground Skraaven in Lofoten in about 68½° N. Lat. This point is at present its most northern limit; although I do not doubt that on further investigation it will be found in the arctic zone much further towards the pole. Its distribution in a southern direction extends at least to the coasts of Ireland, where it was taken during the expedition of the „Porcupine" in the year 1869. Already in the previous year it had been found during the expedition of the „Lightning" in a much more northern locality, namely between Scotland and the Færoe islands. Its distribution as at present known thus extends through no less than 15° of Latitude. The other species Br. endecacnemos seems to have a still greater distribution. It was found during the 2nd expedition of the „Porcupine" off the coast of Portugal. Its most northern locality is Floro 15 miles (94 miles Eng.) north of Bergen, where 2 years ago I took up a perfect specimen. According to this different distribution of both species, it appears that there is some ground for supposing the Brisinga coronata to be on the whole a more northern form than the Br. endecacnemos, which also seems to be confirmed by the physical conditions under which both species are found.

b. Vertical distribution.

The specimens which I have examined of the present species of Brisinga were all taken from about the same depth, namely 250—300 fathoms. Nevertheless it goes, as has been proved, considerably further down into the deep. In the Faroe channel it was taken form a depth of 500 fathoms; and off the west coast of Ireland it was found at the depth of even 800 fathoms. In all probability 200 fathoms must be considered as its highest limit. Whether it goes even lower than 800 fathoms, is not yet certainly decided; but yet it seems to me very probable that it goes at least as deep as the other species Br. ende-cacnemos, which off the Portuguese coast has been taken in 1000 fathoms. The highest limit for this last species seems to be about the same as for Br. coronata, namely about 200 fathoms.

c. External conditions of existence.
Special occurrence.

All my specimens of Brisinga coronata were taken at a considerable distance from the shelving bank of the coast, on an even and flat bottom covered with a more or less thick layer of clay or mud. It appears to have been taken under the same conditions during the atlantic expeditions; but the occurrence of the other species seems to be very dissimilar. It has been always found by Asbjörnsen, as well as by myself, only nearer to the coast on the steep bank which rises from the deeps outside, where the bottom is rocky or stony without any deposit of mud or sand. Whether this dissimilarity in occurrence between the two species is the same everywhere, I do not venture to say; as this is not sufficiently clear from the reports of the atlantic expeditions which we possess. But on our coast the conditions appear to be perfectly constant. The temperature in which the Br. coronata lives at Lofoten is, according to the investigations made by me in the summer of 1869, about + 4° C.; but it is necessary to remark that I had at the time only a very imperfect deep-sea thermometer at my disposal. It is thus very possible that the temperature may have been in reality somewhat lower, which would also agree with the statement of temperature communicated in the report on the „Lightning's" expedition. It occurred, according to this report, only in the cold area in the Faroe channel, where the temperature, at the depth of 500 fathoms, was only a little above the freezing point. Off the west coast of Ireland it seems however to have been taken by Jeffreys in a much higher bottom-temperature. It appears nevertheless from other circumstances of the animal's occurrence here, that the Fauna exhibited on the whole a decidedly northern character. In Lofoten it was found together with Astropecten Andromeda and tennispinus, Echinus norvegicus, Stichopus natans, an enormous number of Ulocyathus arcticus, various Molluses, among which Admete viridula, Trophon barvicensis,

72

Dentalium agile and Neæra obesa were the most numerous, and with various Annelides and Crustacea. It occurred chiefly in a single confined area, at the distance of about 1 Norwegian mile from land, but here in quite unusual abundance. In one single haul I once got up in the dredge no less than 5 more or less perfect specimens. As often as I removed a little from that place, which could only be found with great trouble, by reason of its great distance from the shore, the specimens became immediately very scarce. Whether this particular spot on the bottom of the sea offered any specially favorable points for the thriving of the species, I have not been able to ascertain. I should be more inclined to presume that this congregation of individuals was only temporary, and mainly to be considered as connected with the propagation of the species taking place just at that time.

Remarks on Homology and Affinity.

(Philosophy).

A. General Homology.

1.

On the scientific significance of the genus Brisinga, considered from the stand-point of the Darwinian theory.

When we now, after having gone through the natural history of this remarkable star-fish, finally review the most important features of its organisation, we shall certainly be forced to acknowledge that its structure is in reality by no means so entirely anomalous as its very peculiar external appearance might induce us to suppose, and as it has indeed been hitherto considered; for we can now, without any hesitation whatever, assign to it its systematic place in the order of the Asteriæ or star-fishes, without being forced to regard it as a connecting link between the Asteriæ and the Ophiuræ. Nevertheless this star-fish exhibits in its structure some highly remarkable and significant peculiarities, which can not but lead us to several reflexions on the Asterides in general, and on their relation to other Echinoderms; and we shall hereby come quite naturally to the important question of the relation of the whole type of Echinoderms to other animal types. It is also now my opinion that this remarkable star-fish opens to us on many points a clearer view of the nature of the Echinoderms than we can hitherto have had. Still it is, here as everywhere, only by Darwin's reformed theory of descent, that these reflexions can bring us to more general, and therefore also in a scientific point of view more important conclusions. Without Darwin's theory we should only see in the Brisinga an abnormally developed star-fish, which in a remarkable and inexplicable manner seems to depart from the conventional type of Echinoderms (the radiary hemispherical form) thereby, as it were, forming one of the extreme points of possible modification within the limits of the type. In regarding the matter from the stand point of the Darwinian doctrine, our reflexions take quite a different direction and

10

a wider range; and we come also to a very different result with respect to the relation of the genus Brisinga to the other Echinoderms. With Darwin's doctrine in view, we can not imagine the type of Echinoderms as anything perfectly defined and given from the very first; but we must imagine this type, like the other higher animal types, as having been produced through successive divergent developments of lower animal forms. We have therefore first and foremost to examine the relation in which the type of Echinoderms stands to the lower animal forms known to us, and seek to discover which of these may be considered as the starting point for the series of developments observed in the Echinoderms. To settle this important point, it is first expedient to decide which of the now living Echinoderm-forms may be presumed to have undergone the least change, and therefore may be considered as the oldest or the most original forms. For the solution of this question Palæontology will naturally furnish the most important data. The first Echinoderms which occur, are those in which we may expect to find the phylogenetic origin of the type best illustrated. For a long time it has been supposed that the Crinoidæ or stone-lillies were the oldest Echinoderms, and especially the so-called Cystideæ which already appeared in great number in the palæolithic time. It appears however on more recent examination, that the Asterides are of still much greater antiquity, for which reason we may also consider this group of Echinoderms as the oldest, from which all the other groups of Echinoderms have been developed. Of the now living Asteridæ, those forms may be considered as the eldest or least changed, which in their habitus agree most with the first forms of remote antiquity. This is now precisely the case with the Brisinga, in a greater degree than with any of the other known star-fishes.

Its habitual resemblance to the oldest known star-fish Protaster is unmistakable; and Asbjörnsen has already drawn attention to this important point. Several other circumstances will now confirm us in the opinion that we have before us in the Brisinga a very ancient form, an isolated surviving representative of the Echinoderms of primitive times, which, confined to the great depths of the ocean, where the physical circumstances have been in all times somewhat similar, has managed in undisturbed peace to preserve the original structure, without requiring to keep pace with the remarkably extensive transformation and diversity of development observed in the Echinoderms generally, and specially in the Asterides. Now the Asterides being, as already stated, considered as the oldest race of Echinoderms, from which the other types of Echinoderms have only been ramified in later times, the genus Brisinga acquires a double importance, as the starting point for a correct appreciation of the nature of the Echinoderms and of their relation to other animal types.

2.

Of the fundamental form of the Echinoderms and of their morphological individuality as illustrated in the genus Brisinga.

As is well known, Cuvier referred the Zoophytes and Echinoderms to one and the same animal type, the so-called radiates; and he has been also followed in this respect by the American naturalist (Agassiz) while here in Europe. We have generally adopted the views first developed by Leuckart, according to which both these groups are sharply distinguished from each other as belonging to essentially different original types. It was the radiary primitive form presumed to be common to both groups, which Cuvier laid so much stress on; and the American naturalists have also held this characteristic to be of such prominent importance, that they still consider the Zoophytes and the Echinoderms, in spite of the many essential differences in their organisation, as belonging to one and the same animal type. If however we follow the method of investigation above indicated, according to which we must take the Asterides, and among these especially the genus Brisinga, as the most original or least changed form of star-fish, for our type, and from this point of view institute our comparison between the Zoophytes and the Echinoderms, we shall find that in reality there is a very essential difference between the strictly radiary structure of the former and the so-called radiary structure in the star-fish, a difference which is of so vital importance that we cannot do otherwise than reopen the question which might seem to have been settled long ago, namely whether the Echinoderms, when all is considered, can be held to be real radiates in the same sense as the Zoophytes. If we now examine the so-called rays or arms in the proper star-fishes, from which again all the other Echinoderms may naturally be derived, we shall find at first that they exhibit a far greater self-sufficiency, a far more self-contained organisation than we ever can find in the Zoophytes, a fact which in the Brisinga is more prominently evident than in any of the other known Echinoderms. While in other Asterides there is always found a more or less strongly developed central section or disc, this is in the Brisinga so extraordinarily reduced, that the whole body may be said to consist of a certain number of arms connected at the base. If we further consider a ray or arm of a star-fish by itself, we shall find that besides exhibiting a perfect bilateral symmetry, it consists of a series of consecutive joints or sections (metamera), a division which is not only expressed in the ambulacral skeleton, but also in most of the other organic systems. If we as formerly, consider the arms of the star-fishes to be real corresponding parts (antimera) analogous to the antimera of Zoophytes, we come to the paradoxical result that an antimeron can be composed of metamera, which according to Häckel [1] is the next highest order of individuality. On the other hand the matter is explained

[1] Generelle Morphologie der Organismen.

in a natural manner, if we regard the rays of the star-fishes not as real antimera, but as morphological individuals of the 5th order, or persons.

The whole star-fish may be thus properly regarded as a colony (cormus) a collection of articulated persons which have arranged themselves in a radiary form round a common centre, and here formed for themselves a common ingestive aperture, in the same manner as the individuals of the Botryllus colonies arrange themselves radially, and form for themselves a common egestive aperture. But as in the case of other colonially organised animals, we do not define the original form according to the form of the colony itself, but according to the structure of the constituent individual animals or persons, so we come, in the case of the star-fishes, to the result that the fundamental form of these animals is not the radiate form, but the bilateral symmetrical (eudipleural), and that the apparently radiate structure is of secondary origin produced by concrescence of a number of eudipleural persons arranged around a common centre. In this manner the last reason would fall away for the union (in itself so unnatural) of the Zoophytes and Echinoderms under one and the same animal type. We might as well consider the star-shaped Botryllus colonies among the Ascidiæ as radiate animals; which probably no one at present would think of doing.

If we accept the above theory (first clearly formulated by Häckel) of the compound structure of the Echinoderms, as properly representing complexes of animals or cormi, it must be admitted that this cormus in the Brisinga is less centralised than in any other Echinoderms; the arms (in this case according to Häckel persons) — as well by their considerable size and loose connexion with the insignificant disc, as by their possessing besides the other organic systems, also a perfect apparatus of generation with corresponding genital apertures — exhibiting an independence that is without parallel in any other Echinoderm. In examining a Brisinga it will therefore be much easier to recognise a real colony or complex of animals, than in examining most other Echinoderms, where the already far advanced centralisation of the cormus undeniably makes such recognition in many cases very difficult. The preponderance of the arms over the insignificant disc, is in the Brisinga so great, that the conception hitherto prevailing of the disc in star-fishes as representing the principal part of the body, of which the arms are only radiating expansions, must here be completely reversed: as we must necessarily consider the arms in the Brisinga as the principal parts, to which the disc only stands in the relation of a sort of appendage. It has also been previously stated, that I have been able to convince myself by direct experiments, that the single arms of the Brisinga, detached from the disc, continue to live and to exercise their ordinary vital functions, even long after the disc itself has ceased to live; and that there is likewise a very great probability for their being capable, under favorable circumstances, of continuing their life, each for itself, and little by little reproducing the other parts belonging to a complete colony, the disc as well as the rest: I have even felt bound to state, as something which has the highest degree of probability for it, that such a successive detachment of the arms takes place in the normal state as a voluntary act of the animal, conducive to non-sexual propagation (by divisio radialis).

There is another feature in the species of Brisinga here noticed which is worthy of remark, as essentially supporting the theory above developed; and that is the contrast to the real radiates (Zoophytes), in the great inconstancy of the number of the rays (arms), which even makes it very difficult to decide what number shall be considered as normal or typical. A similar, although certainly not so extensive, inconstancy is found only in some few forms within the group of star-fishes, which we must consider as the oldest and most original Echinoderms. Thus the number of arms varies not a little in our two species of Solaster, as also in several exotic forms of the genus Asterias, Luidia, Ophidiaster. In most of the star-fishes however the number of arms has with the increasing centralisation of the cormus become fixed at the number which is typical for the Echinoderms, namely five. The same is the case with the Ophiuræ, which stand next to the star-fishes, where in like manner the number five, with very few exceptions (some species of the genera Ophiacantha, Ophiactis and Ophiothela with 6 arms) is completely constant; and in the 2 most divergent groups of Echinoderms, Echinoids and Holothurians, in which the centralisation of the body has attained its highest degree, not a single instance is to be found of deviation from the normal number of five ambulacra. It is also only in these groups that, collaterally with the complete concrescence of the single individuals (persons) originally composing the body, new and peculiar relationships appear, which seem still more to disguise the original polymerous composition. Thus we see in the so-called irregular Echinides (Spatangus) and in divers Holothuriæ (Psolus), that there proceeds from the whole cormus, by means of one of the sides acting as a sort of creeping disc, (the ventral side) an apparently single bilaterally symmetrical individual; and in the footless Holothuriæ (Synapta) where proper ambulacrals are wanting, the last remnant of the complex character has disappeared, and the whole body seems even to return to the lowest (monaxonous) fundamental forms. If we consider one of these anomalous forms by itself, it will certainly be difficult to recognise in it any real complex or cormus. But if we go through the whole series of Echinoderms, we shall soon see that there can be no question of any other than phenomena of secondary adaptation; and these abnormal relations can therefore by no means disprove the above noticed theory of the original composition of the body of the Echinoderms, as derived from the oldest and most original forms of star-fishes.

3.

On the phylogenetic relationship of the Echinoderms to other animal types.

If we accept the theory noticed in the preceding paragraph with respect to the composite individuality of the Echinoderms for which, as will be shewn, the examination of the Brisinga seems to afford essential support, we shall quite naturally come to judge of the generic relationship of the Echinoderms to other animal types in a very different manner from heretofore. We thus see in the star-fishes the most original and least altered Echinoderms, which therefore must be selected as the starting point for our comparison with other animal types. Moreover it is not the whole body of the star-fish, but the single rays or arms which must here form the subject of our investigations; as these rays or arms do properly represent the original echinoderm individuals or persons. We have in the first place before us a completely bilaterally symmetrical body, with a dorsal and a ventral side, right and left side, oral and aboral extremity, the interior organs of which shew the same strict symmetry. Next we shall find that these internal organs have a fixed regular and peculiar position relatively to each other; below, the central parts of the nervous system; then, the vascular system with the parts appertaining to it; then, the perivisceral cavity with the digestive system and organs of generation contained therein; and externally, the skin, consisting of 2 distinct layers, the interior muscular, and the exterior cellular. We find moreover that this body exhibits a series of consecutive similar sections or metamera, not only expressed in the skeleton but also in several of the interior organic systems; the muscular system, the nervous system, the vascular system. These are all things which we only find again in the great race of the articulata and particularly in the worms (Vermes). We are naturally led hereby to the conclusion that the nearest relations of the Echinoderms are not, as hitherto generally supposed, the Zoophytes, but the Vermes; and that this last ancient and extensively ramified trunk, in which we trace, as it were, the very first rough sketches of all the higher animal types (even including the vertebrata) must also be regarded as the trunk from which the Echinoderms, although apparently of a very different fundamental structure, have had their origin. This theory of the phylogenetic development of the Echinoderms, which is likewise most sharply and most clearly represented by Häckel, acquires also an essential support from the Brisinga, the so-called rays or arms of which exhibit more evidently than in any other Echinoderm a worm-like appearance, and the great self-sufficiency of which is not only expressed in the exterior, but also in the interior organisation; for, as has been already observed, even the organs of generation, which else, at least in great part, are confined to the central section or disc, are here entirely separated from the same, and symmetrically imbedded in the cavity of the arms. The relationship of the Echinoderms to the Vermes has indeed long ago been recognised by some naturalists;

although certainly other views have partially prevailed. That some Holothuriæ (Synapta) in their exterior habitus, have a striking resemblance to worms, is a well-known fact, and has given rise to the popular denomination „worm-cucumbers". We have likewise a peculiar class among the Vermes, the so-called trunk-worms (Gephyrea), the organisation of which exhibits several remarkable points of resemblance with the Holothurians, and therefore also has formerly been referred to the type of the Echinoderms. Since however, as above stated, we have in the Holothuriæ really the most divergently developed group of Echinoderms, it cannot actually be here that we should seek for the original ancestry of the Echinoderms; although it can not be denied that we may also here observe a remarkable retrogression to the same type which may be assumed as basis for the oldest and most original Echinoderms, the star-fishes.

In opposition to the theory above stated as to the phylogenetic relationship of the Echinoderms to the Articulata, the ambulacral or water-system has been adduced as presumably exclusively peculiar to the Echinoderms. It can certainly not be denied that this organic system affords, by its extremely peculiar and complicated development and functions, one of the most distinctive characteristics of the Echinoderms; but it is by no means on that account decided that nothing of the kind is to be found in other animal types. We have frequent instances of one and the same organic system developing itself in different groups of animals in a very different manner, and exercising quite dissimilar functions; so that the originally common fundamental form may be difficult to recognise. We have in the Vermes a very extensive organic system in the form of tortuous canals, opening partly externally partly in the cavity of the body, and appearing decidedly in certain cases to be water-ducts; while in other cases they have secretory functions. Where the body is evidently devided into segments, these vessels appear to be arranged symmetrically in each segment, and have therefore in the annelides been indifferently denominated segmental organs. It may be assumed that we have here the analogon of the ambulacral system in the Echinoderms; at least it appears to me that there cannot be adduced any decided proof to the contrary. There is another characteristic which seems to be foreign to the Vermes, and which is so prominent in the Echinoderms that even the whole type has derived its name therefrom, namely the cuticular skeleton more or less strongly developed by calcareous secretions, to which we may add that in the Asterides and Crinoides there is even another sort of interior skeleton which exhibits a so striking habitual ressemblance to the vertebral column in the Vertebrata that the single segments even bear the same name (vertebræ). In examining the real Vermes we certainly do not find anything analogous; but this characteristic is by no means foreign to the whole tribe of Articulata. In the Crustaceans we have frequent instances of the integuments, by absorbing lime, assuming quite as firm a consistency as in the Echinoderms; and by interior processes of this cuticular armor, there is also formed here (Decapods) a sort of interior skeleton, which serves partly for the insertion of the limbs with their muscles, and partly also as support for interior organic systems (the nervous system). That the ambulacral skeleton in the Asterides, in spite of its habitual resemblance, has no analogy whatever with the vertebral column in the Vertebrata, but properly belongs to the cuticular skeleton — is satisfactorily ascertained, and is clearly evidenced (inter alia) by its development being perfectly conformable to that of the cuticular skeleton.

We have not yet touched on a point which, just where there is a question of phylogenetic relations, must occupy a very important place, and will often alone be able to give us the most certain and significant indication in this respect: I mean the history of development. We shall find also in considering this important part of the natural history of the Echinoderms, an essential support for the theory above noticed; at the same time as many hitherto quite unintelligible points connected with the subject will, by help of this theory, find a natural explanation. As is well known, most Echinoderms go through a most remarkable and peculiar metamorphosis, which has first been made the subject of particular and minute research by the celebrated German naturalist Johannes Müller. From the egg there proceeds a creature of most romantic appearance, furnished with various lobes and processes, swimming away by means of sinuous bands of cilia, and having no resemblance whatever to the respective Echinoderm, being a perfectly bilaterally symmetrical animal, which according to its whole structure would most naturally be referred to the group of Vermes, and which also exhibits a striking resemblance to the so-called larvæ of certain Nemertina and Gephyrea. Only at a later period, there is laid, in a limited part of the interior of this worm-like animal, the foundation of the future echinoderm; and as the latter is developed, the original so-called larva-body shrivels up little by little or becomes resorbed. There is much to forbid considering this peculiar process of development as a real metamorphosis. It is indeed usual for the whole larva-body to be resorbed, or as it were taken up in the formation of the Echinoderm; but we have still instances of this not being always the case. Thus the Bipinnaria-larva continues to swim about even after the young star-fish has detached itself; and it may even be imagined possible that such a larva can again give origin to a new star-fish. This instance alone is sufficient to distinguish very sharply the development of the Echinoderms from the ordinary development by metamorphosis. We must on the contrary bring it under the great law of alternate generation, as a peculiar modification of the same, chiefly characterised by the cycle of generation being, as far as we yet know, only represented by 2 Bionta. It is this form of alternate generation which has been called by Hackel, Metagenesis successiva. We have consequently in the peculiar so-called Echinoderm-larva properly speaking not an incomplete stage of development, but one of the 2 fully developed alternating generations, namely the non sexual generation. The apparently paradoxical and unintelligible fact that the 2 Bionta in the same cycle of generation are constructed in totally different fundamental forms, one in the radiary and the other in the bilaterally symmetrical (eudiplemrous) form, can only find its natural explanation, if we consider the developed Echinoderm as an individual of a higher order, or a colony, the apparently corresponding parts or antimera of which represent the original individuals (persons). Each of these is then, as it were, the individual which represents the sexual generation, constructed according to the bilaterally symmetrical fundamental form, and, as it were, most naturally referable to the class of Vermes. The so-called development of the Echinoderms in the body of the larva, must then be considered as a sort of budding of several worm-like individuals, which arrange themselves radially round a common centre, and, by concrescence of their oral extremities, form an individual of a higher order, a colony or a complex of animals. A rather analogous case has already long been known in the Salpæ, in which similarly the 2 alternating generations represent morphological individuals of different orders: the non-sexual generation always consisting of single individuals (persons), which again, by budding, produce in their interior coherent complexes of individuals, or colonies (the so-called Salpæ-chains) representing the sexual generation. If we examine the manner in which an arm or ray is reproduced de novo in an otherwise developed star-fish, we shall similarly find cases which decidedly remind us of the Vermes. The various joints or metamera are formed, as already noticed above, successively from the base of the extreme first-formed joint, exactly in the same manner as the joints of a tapeworm-chain, or like the segments of a nascent annelide. We come thus, in considering the history of the development of the Echinoderms in general, to the same result to which the minute investigation of the organisation in a fully developed star-fish has already led us. The theory already set up by Duvernoy, afterwards developed in greater detail by Huxley, and recently finally elucidated by Haeckel, as to the composite individuality of the Echinoderms and their phylogenetic connexion with the Vermes, — which theory was formerly generally regarded as a wild fancy — must in reality, on more minute examination, be recognised as having very much to support it; and so much the more, as we hereby obtain a quite unexpected explanation of some hitherto very obscure cases in the natural history of the Echinoderms.

4.

On the genealogical relation of the several groups of Echinoderms to each other.

We have above considered the proper star-fishes as the oldest, or original Echinoderms, from which therefore all the other Echinoderms may be derived. We are led to assume this in advance, quite simply by the fact that the star-fishes are, so far as we know, of all the Echinoderms those which go furthest back in time, namely to the sub-silurian formation. This assumption is also in the best harmony with the above-noticed theory of the composite individuality and phylogenetic relations of the Echinoderms. If we consider the Echinoderms as original cormi or complexes of vermicular individuals, it is clear that those forms must be the oldest or least changed, in which this cormus exhibits the least degree of centralisation, and in which therefore the component individuals (persons) evidently shew their original self-sufficiency as such. This is precisely the case with the star-fishes, the rays or arms of which give, each for itself, a complete image of the whole organisation. Among the star-fishes again, it is the genus Brisinga which in this respect most distinguishes itself; for which reason we must thus consider this form as the oldest or most original of all the Echinoderms. To prevent misunderstanding, it must be expressly remarked that this refers chiefly to the general combination of the body, not to the organisation in its details. In this respect the Brisinga is in exact conformity, as has been shewn, with the star-fishes now living; and it cannot fairly be assumed that these have been able to preserve unchanged the self-same organisation of the ancient worm-like creatures from which the whole tribe of Echinoderms proceeds.

In the genealogical development of the tribe of Echinoderms, which may be supposed to have progressed uninterruptedly in the immense periods during which the animals hereto belonging have existed upon the earth, there appears chiefly to be manifested a tendency towards greater and greater centralisation of the originally independent individuals composing the cormus. The Echinoderms in which this has been in the highest degree successful are undoubtedly the Holothurians; and these must therefore be considered as the newest, most divergently developed and most altered Echinoderms; this conclusion is also corroborated by Paleontology; as we do not find any traces of these animals until the Jura period; while all the other groups of Echinoderms are referred to far earlier times. Between the 2 extreme points, the Asteriæ and Holothuriæ, there are a great number of in some cases widely divergent series of developments, all of which may however be naturally referred to the Asteriæ as the proper fundamental forms. In examining the various groups of Echinoderms, we shall find that the said tendency in the cormus, after this is centralised as an independent physiological individual, takes 2 courses, both leading to the same end, although in rather different manners: both are already partially indicated in the group of Asteroidea, but only come to their full manifestation, on the one side in the Echinoids and Holothurians, and on the other side in the Ophiurans and Crinoids.

One course consists in more or less extensive concrescence of the individuals (the rays, antimera) originally connected only by their oral extremities, whereby the central connecting part or disc gains in circumference, as it were, at the expense of the arms, which at last seem entirely to disappear or to be absorbed in the disc. This change is manifested chiefly in the exterior, without, at least in the commencement, being accompanied by any corresponding alteration of the interior organisation. Only at a later period there occur other alterations, chiefly those connected with the digestive system, the main parts of which, originally belonging to each single individual (person), after being thus brought mechanically nearer together, at last undergo a transformation more convenient for the alimentation of the whole colony. Among the known star-fishes now living, we have numerous instances of such a centralisation manifested in the exterior. Between the forms provided with long arms and particularly small discs (Asterias, Pedicellaster &c.) and the short-armed star-fishes (Porania Pterasters) in which the arms are only insignificant processes of the powerfully developed disc, we have all possible transitions. At last the arms appear to be entirely wanting and only indicated by the pentagonal form of the disc (Goniaster) nay, in the genus Culcita even the angulosity of the disc is indistinct: and we have here before us a disc-like body in which only the 5 ambulacrals still indicate the original arms or persons. The further change next consists in an incipient diminution of the antiambulacral area, whereby the ambulacral area, originally confined to the ventral side, gains a constantly greater and greater extension over the surface of the body; until at last the antiambulacral area is still only visible as an insignificant space on the superior pole. In the periphery of this space, there lie, in the regular Echinoids, the 5 peculiar ocellary plates with their pigmentary spots, exactly corresponding to the organs of sight situated in many star-fishes at the extremity of the arms, whence again it appears that we have in the ocellary plates the counterpart of the extreme arm-joints of the star-fishes. In several Echinoids the body exhibits moreover a very evident pentagonal form as indication of the original 5 arms. In like manner we have among the Echinoids many forms in which the body is quite as disc-like as in the star-fishes. Between these flat Echinoids and the high hemispherical, including the pyramidal forms, we have all the transitions. If we imagine the high pyramidal form still further developed in the same direction, it is not difficult to derive the cylindrical form, which we find in the Holothurians. Here also the originally ventral (ambulacral) side occupies the whole surface of the body; and of the antiambulacral area every trace has disappeared. The peculiar development of the water-feet situated nearest to the mouth of the Holothurians into capturing arms, is, like the complicated dental apparatus of the Echinoids, of secondary origin: just as we can also see in the peculiar apparently bilateral symmetry of the irregular Echinoids and of certain Holothurians (Psolus) only formations determined by particular processes of adaptation.

The other course of development, which likewise leads to considerable centralisation of the cormus, is not properly speaking accompanied by any extensive concrescence of the original individuals (arms, rays) while it is here essentially an internal transformation which from the first takes place, a dislocation of the internal organic systems, whereby their principal parts retract themselves, as it were, from their original place in the arms to the centre of the colony, or to the disc, which hereby becomes the most essential and most organised part; while the original individuals, the arms, are reduced to the rank of mere organs. The organic system first acted on is also in this case the digestive system, the most important really digesting sections of which in the star-fishes have still their original place in the cavities of the arms as the so-called radial cæca, but which, in the course of development here treated of, centralise themselves little by little in the cavity of the disc itself. This

11*

becomes possible by means of a peculiar development of the antiambulacral side of the disc which hereby, quite contrarily to what is the case in the other course of development, acquires a preponderance over the ambulacral side; a phenomenon especially manifested in the Crinoids, in which the so-called calix, with the articulated stem proceeding from the same, is attributable to such a development. In connexion with this centralisation of the digestive system, there stands also a centralisation of another organic system, namely the blood-system; as the cavities of the arms become at the same time narrower and narrower; so that the perivisceral blood-cavity is likewise, for the greater part, limited to the disc. We may already see evident signs of the centralisation referred to in real star-fishes, namely in the remarkable fossil form Protaster; but we do not see the full development of it until we come to the Ophiurans and Crinoids, in which the arms, by the above-mentioned reduction of 2 of the most important organic systems, have lost so much of their original independence, that they have become mere appendices of the disc, or simple organs. The greatest centralisation of the cormus attained in this manner, is probably exhibited in the Ophiurans and in their relatives the Euryalæ, in which one more important organic system has abandoned its original place in the arms and centralised itself in the cavity of the disc, namely the generative organs. But in the Crinoids these organs are still quite separate from the disc; for which reason we must also consider these Echinoderms as less completely centralised than the Ophiurans, and therefore of more ancient origin, which is also in some degree indicated by the rather variable number of arms in the sea-lilies; and we are likewise led by palæontological deductions to the same conclusion; as evident Ophiurans do not occur until long after the Crinoids; although the course of development which seems to tend towards the ophiurean type is found manifested at a very early period, namely in the ancient star-fish Protaster. The articulated stem peculiar to the Crinoids must be assumed to be a characteristic acquired at an early period in consequence of special conditions of existance, and continued in the younger stage even in the Antedon, which is free when fully developed. The genus Antedon must therefore, in spite of its habitual resemblance to the Euryalæ among the Ophiuridæ, be considered as a further developed divergent branch of the genuine Crinoids.

It is thus evident that in the first course of development, which we are able to trace through the groups of star-fishes, sea-urchins and sea-cucumbers, the centralisation of the body is chiefly manifested in a reduction of the arms brought about by concrescence. In the other course of development we have on the contrary an instance of even further development of the arms, without however any decentralisation of the cormus taking place. This further development of the arms may consist partly in an increased reproduction of joints or metamera, whereby the arms may often attain a really extraordinary length in proportion to the diameter of the disc (for instance in the genera Amphiura and Ophiopeltis belonging to the Ophiuridæ) and it may consist partly in a ramification of the arms, which may either be a more or less extensive dichotomic splitting, or a development of alternating lateral branches (Pinnulæ); of both these sorts of ramification we have instances in the Crinoids, and of an extremely extensive dichotomic splitting in the Euryalæ. In these last the arms may be said to have attained a stronger development in this direction than in any other Echinoderm. Nevertheless such a Euryala with its widely ramified arms, the mass of which surpasses many times the mass of the disc, is far more centralised than even the most short-armed star-fishes. As regards the fossil groups Blastoidea and Cystidea these are most nearly related, as divergent branches, to the Crinoids. The arms have here apparently undergone, by some peculiar processes of adaptation, a retrograde development. We may perhaps so far most properly consider them as degenerate Crinoids, just as the footless sea-cucumbers (Synapta) may be supposed to be degenerate Holothurians.

The genealogical relationship of the various groups of Echinoderms to each other may henceforth, with special regard to the various modes of centralisation of the cormus, be graphically represented as follows:

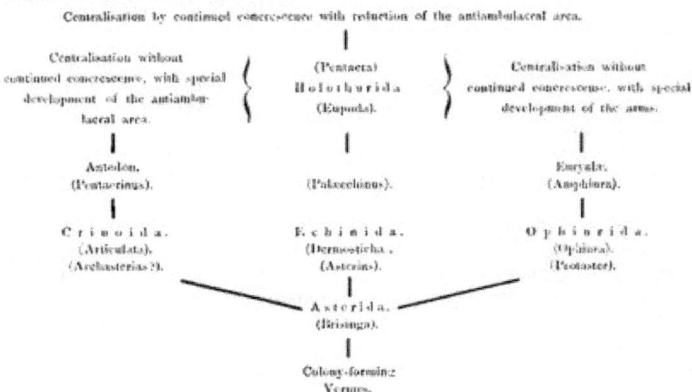

Centralisation by continued concrescence with reduction of the antiambulacral area.

Centralisation without continued concrescence, with special development of the antiambulacral area.	(Pentacta) Holothurida (Eupoda).	Centralisation without continued concrescence, with special development of the arms.
Antedon. (Pentacrinus).	(Palæechinus).	Euryalæ. (Amphiura).
C r i n o i d a. (Articulata). (Archasterias?).	E c h i n i d a. (Dermostieha. (Asterias).	O p h i u r i d a. (Ophiura). (Pteraster).

A s t e r i d a. (Brisinga).

Colony-forming Vermes.

5.

Of the relation of the genus Brisinga to the Asteroidea in general.

After having made the above more general remarks on the organisation of the Echinoderms and their relationship to other animal types, as exemplified in the genus Brisinga, we return more specially to this genus to examine the relation in which it stands to the other known forms of the class Asteroidea. As is well known, the general view has hitherto been that the genus Brisinga formed the type of an entirely separate group or order of Asteroidea (Brisingastra Häckel) which as it were, formed the transition between the Asteridæ and the Ophiuridæ. And to this conclusion we may really be easily led by considering the animal's exterior habitus. But we shall now, after having become better acquainted with the organisation of this remarkable form, be forced to come to an entirely different result. Its relationship to the Ophiuridæ is in reality very distant; while its conformity with the proper star-fishes (Asteridæ) in all essential characteristic points is so great, that in spite of its anomalous appearance, it must take its place in this order. In illustration of this I will here briefly point out the characteristics whereby it connects itself with the Asteridæ and distinguishes itself from the Ophiuridæ.

1) The considerable and variable number of arms in the Brisinga has only its parallel in certain Asteridæ; while the number of arms in the Ophiuridæ, in conformity with the advanced centralisation, has mostly already become permanent as the typical number for the Echinoderms 5.

2) The ambulacral skeleton is in the Brisinga in its main features constructed exactly according to the same type as in the proper star-fishes and differs essentially from the ambulacral skeleton of the Ophiuridæ.

3) Also the cuticular skeleton shews a much greater conformity with the Asteridæ than with the Ophiuridæ, and especially the connecting calcareous ribs over the basal section of the arms are entirely foreign to the Ophiuridæ; while it is easy to recognise in them the analogon of the wide-meshed calcareous net found in the skin of many Asteridæ.

4) Pedicellariæ are never observed in Ophiuridæ, while we find them in many Asteridæ of a very similar structure to those of the Brisinga.

5) The structure of the madreporic body and its dorsal situation characterise the Brisinga as a genuine Asteride.

6) Likewise the wide and deep ambulacral furrows, which are never found in the Ophiuridæ, where, on the contrary, the ventral side of the arms is covered with peculiar cuticular plates (ventral plates).

7) The water-feet of the Brisinga correspond in their strong development, and in their whole structure, completely to those of the star-fishes; and especially we do not know any Ophiuridæ in which they terminate in a clearly developed sucker.

8) Neither do we find in the Ophiuridæ any separate Ampullæ for the water-feet; while these Ampullæ are in the Brisinga developed precisely in the same manner as in the proper star-fishes.

9) The perivisceral cavity is in the Ophiuridæ confined to the disc only; while the arms represent solid parts only containing a narrow canal for the reception of the radial

water-vessel and the radial nerve. In the Brisinga on the contrary, the perivisceral cavity extends, as in the Asteridæ, through the whole length of the arms between the ambulacral skeleton and the dorsal skin, containing in its basal part various internal organs.

10) Radial continuations of the digestive system (radial cæca) are never found in the Ophiuridæ; while in the Brisinga they are developed precisely in the same manner as in the Asteridæ.

11) No special masticatory-apparatus (teeth, dental papillæ) are to be found in the Brisinga any more than in other Asteridæ. But on the other hand the furrow-spines situated on the interior contiguous adambulacral plates assume a particular development, just as in other star-fishes, forming the so-called oral spines.

12) The organ of secretion noticed in the Brisinga, with its issue on the dorsal side of the disc, is something which we find only in the proper star-fishes.

13) The so-called „heart", to which nothing corresponding has yet been noticed in the Ophiurans, agrees, in its structure and in its relation to the other parts, entirely with the same organ in the Asteridæ, as is the case also with the situation and structure of the stone canal.

14) As the organs of generation in the Brisinga are confined to the arms only, we do not of course find the genital fissures on the lower side of the disc which characterise the Ophiuridæ.

15) The terminal organs of sense in the Brisinga find their most complete homologon in the Asteridæ; while nothing corresponding is found in the Ophiuridæ.

16) The manner in which the Brisinga moves, is the same as in the Asteridæ; that is to say, essentially by the play of the water-feet only; and not as in the Ophiuridæ by the flexion of the arms.

Considering all these important characteristics, the points of agreement with the Ophiuridæ which the Brisinga exhibits, namely the little rounded disc plainly distinguished from the long thin arms, and the absence of cuticular pores and cuticular tentacles (respiratory tubes), must go for nothing.

In order still better to understand the great conformity of the genus Brisinga with the proper star-fishes, we will once again briefly consider some of the most important organs in the Brisinga, and institute a detailed comparison with the same in other star-fishes. We will dwell chiefly on the solid calcareous parts which support the body and determine its form.

a. Homology of the ambulacral skeleton.
(Tab. V).

We have previously divided the ambulacral skeleton of the Brisinga into 2 parts: the skeleton of the disc, and the skeleton of the arms; and this is so far correct, as the skeleton of the disc in the Brisinga really forms a connected whole, a solid calcareous frame, to the exterior side of which the skeleton of the arms is attached. It has been however shewn that this frame is actually composed of the same elements as the ambulacral skeleton of the arms, namely of 2 sets of ambulacral vertebræ, in a line with the series of vertebræ in the arms, and properly representing the interior-continuation of these series. It has likewise been shewn that the exterior set of vertebræ in very young specimens, come out of their connexion with the oral ring, and thereby evidently connect themselves immediately with the skeleton of the arm. Properly therefore there remains in the skeleton of the disc only a single set of vertebræ, connected with each other by interposed calcareous plates, so as to form a connected ring which surrounds the oral aperture.

If we now examine how the case stands in other star-fishes, we shall also find that the proper ambulacral skeleton of the disc forms here only the immediate continuation of the series of vertebræ of the arms. Only the interior set of vertebræ are in immediate contact, or form a closed calcareous ring round the oral aperture; while the other part of the series of vertebræ, reckoned as belonging to the disc, is only indirectly connected by the skin of the disc and by the calcareous plates imbedded in the same. Accordingly as the arms are longer or shorter, the number of vertebræ entering into the composition of the disc is extremely variable in the various star-fishes. In certain forms (Goniaster, Culcita) where the arms are only indicated by obtuse angles, the whole ambulacral skeleton may properly be said to be absorbed in the disc; in the long-armed star-fishes, for instance Asterias, the part of the ambulacral skeleton belonging to the disc is, on the other hand, only insignificant; while the greater part belongs to the arms. Between these extreme points, we find again all possible transitions. It is now easy to see that the skeleton of the disc in the Brisinga can by no means be compared with the whole skeleton of the disc in other star-fishes, but only with its innermost part (the interior or the 2 interior sets of vertebræ which immediately surround the mouth). The apparently very anomalous structure of the skeleton of the disc in the Brisinga, will then be found in complete conformity with what we know of other star-fishes; only with the difference that the interior vertebræ are necessarily more firmly and intimately connected together, in order to support the enormously developed arms. In Tab. V, fig. 1 & 2 there is represented the oral ring of a 9-armed specimen of Brisinga coronata, with the basis of the skeleton of 3 of the arms in natural connection with the disc; and for the sake of comparison, there is also represented in fig. 7 & 8 a corresponding part of the ambulacral skeleton of a likewise 9-armed specimen of Solaster endeca. We shall here recognise homologous parts everywhere. As in the Brisinga, so also in the Solaster and other star-fishes, the interior set of vertebræ acquire a peculiar development; the vertebræ connecting themselves with each other so as to form a sort of oral ring. The connexion takes place here also by means of peculiar connecting plates perfectly corresponding with the 2 sorts of interposed plates in the oral ring of the Brisinga. The wedge-plates especially are plainly developed, without however connecting themselves immovably by suture with the adjacent vertebræ. To their exterior side are attached the radial septa, which in a fan-like arrangement divide the coeloma of the disc; and in these septa there are often developed peculiar calcareous plates, the innermost of which are articulated with the wedge-plate. In one of the radial septa which include the stone-canal and the so-called heart, this calcareous plate is double; and its homology with the first pair of dorsal marginal plates in the Brisinga seems thereby to become highly probable. The so-called parietal plates, which in the Brisinga contribute essentially to form the interior wall of the oral ring, are also found again in the Solaster and other star-fishes. They are however here of much slighter development, and separated from each other by a considerable interval; on the interior side they form a horisontal furrow for the circular ambulacral vessel, limited below by a projecting sharp edge, which completely corresponds to the circular rim projecting inwards on the oral ring in the Brisinga. While in the Brisinga it goes uninterruptedly round the whole interior of the oral ring, in the Solaster and other star-fishes it is interrupted at each vertebra in two places, where the circular ambulacral vessel is only circumcluded by ligaments. In fig. 9 & 10, which represent corresponding parts of the ambulacral skeleton seen from above in the Brisinga and Solaster, the corresponding calcareous plates are indicated by the same letters, in order that their complete resemblance may be more easily observed.

If we now turn the ambulacral skeleton, and view it from the ventral side (fig. 2 & 3), it will likewise be at once evident that in both forms there are everywhere found completely homologous parts. The deep ambulacral furrows, at the bottom of which the median longitudinal furrow for the radiary water-vessels, and the holes placed in pairs for the water-feet are seen, are bounded in both on each side by a row of plates (adambulacral plates), which are connected with each other by elastic muscular bands, and to which the so-called furrow-spines are attached; the innermost of these plates being, in both, united immovably by suture with its neighbors into one continuous piece projecting under the oral ring. To this piece are attached the so-called oral spines directed in fan-like arrangement towards the mouth. That there are apparently in the Brisinga no oral angles to be found, is a consequence of the slighter development of the piece, in connexion with the greater breadth and more solid composition of the oral ring. It will be evident from what has previously been written, that if we imagine the basis of the arms in the Brisinga connected to a certain extent above and below by skin, we shall have a tolerably normally developed star-fish: just as, if we imagine in a Solaster the incisions between the arms continued up to the last ambulacral vertebra but one, we shall obtain a form pretty nearly corresponding to the Brisinga. That the coeloma of the disc in the Brisinga is not continued beyond the oral ring or the innermost contiguous vertebra, and that the dorsal skin attaches itself immediately in the periphery of the oral ring, is again a natural consequence of the reduction of the skeleton of the disc. The interior organs enclosed in the cavity of the disc, the

12

stomach and the apparatus of secretion, are in consequence of this limited to a much smaller space than in other star-fishes, (comp. Tab. VI, fig. 36 & 37).

b. Homology of the skeleton of the skin.

The integuments in the Brisinga exhibit, as well with regard to consistency as to structure, the most complete resemblance to those of the proper star-fishes; and also the calcareous parts belonging to the skin may be referred to corresponding parts in other star-fishes. It has thus been previously shewn that the calcareous parts imbedded in the dorsal skin of the disc, as well as the very peculiar calcareous ribs in the dorsal skin of the arms, can very naturally be referred to the same category as the so-called calcareous net in the skin of other star-fishes. Also with regard to the so-called marginal plates, likewise belonging to the skin, we have in the Brisinga something analogous in the small plates, arranged at the basis of the arms or in the angles of the arms, of which the innermost, connected with the wedge-plates, have, in fully developed specimens, entered into the composition of the oral ring, while the 2 others on each side belong specially to the arms, as evidently developed dorsal marginal plates. Also along the whole of the rest of the arm, there may be noticed, as previously remarked, rudiments of similar dorsal marginal plates, which however in the basal part of the arm go in one with the transversal calcareous ribs, and represent the exterior somewhat enlarged ends of the same. On the other hand, no trace is to be found in the Brisinga of ventral marginal plates; as also, owing to the complete absence of real interbrachial space, there can of course be none of the so-called intermediary ventral plates (interambulacral plates) imbedded in the ventral skin.

c. Homology of the spines.

We find in the Brisinga, as in other star-fishes, dorsal spines, lateral or marginal spines, and so-called furrow-spines; the latter are attached immediately to the ambulacral skeleton (to the ambulacral plates) while the others issue from the calcareous parts developed in the skin.

That the spines in the Brisinga are surrounded by wide cuticular sheaths, seems at first glance to be something quite special and peculiar for this genus. Nevertheless on more minute examination we shall find also in other star-fishes a similar, although slighter and less remarkable cuticular sheath round the spines. Even if this cuticular sheath can not in isolated cases be indicated; it is yet certain that it has originally existed, and has only at a later period been removed.

As to the arrangement of the spines, this will naturally be regulated by the arrangement of the calcareous parts to which they are attached. The different situation of the dorsal spines on the disc and on the arms is quite naturally determined thereby. Of marginal spines there are in the Brisinga only the dorsal, ventral marginal plates being, as previously noticed, entirely wanting. The dorsal marginal spines have however precisely the same arrangement along the sides of the arms as in other star-fishes. The furrow-spines have likewise, apart from their number, on the whole the same arrangement as in other star-fishes, those on each adambulacral plate forming a (certainly not quite regular) transverse row, and those on the innermost contiguous adambulacral plates assuming also in the Brisinga a peculiar form and direction as real oral spines.

d. Homology of the pedicellaries.

The pedicellaries in the Brisinga are of a very similar structure to those of several other star-fishes, for instance Asterias, Pedicellaster. On the other hand they differ by their comparatively insignificant size, their enormous number and their different arrangement. While those of the other star-fishes are more dispersed on the skin, or at most group themselves in some quantity around the base of the larger spines (Asterias) those of the Brisinga are present in enormous numbers on the cuticular sheaths of the spines themselves; and those which are attached immediately on the dorsal skin of the arms are collected, likewise in enormous numbers, into plainly defined transverse stripes, which can even assume the form of semicylindrical transverse ridges (Br. coronata). As regards the general homology of the pedicellaries, their position on the cuticular sheaths of the spines shews clearly enough, that they cannot be, as Agassiz[*] has tried to demonstrate, originally homologous with the spines. These latter are developed from the interior cuticular layer (corium) while the pedicellaries are, as the development also shews, (see above p. 64) exclusively an epidermis-formation. It may indeed in a certain sense be said that the so-called pedicellaries of the Echinidæ are homologous with the spines. But what we call pedicellaries in the Echinidæ are, it must be remembered, essentially different from what we call by that name in the star-fish. A pedicellary of the former is properly a compound organ including a spine, beneath the proper pedicellary, (the so-called stem of the pedicellary): such a pedicellary is in other words a real spine, on the cuticular sheath of which there is only developed one single terminal pedicellary; and it cannot therefore be compared with a single pedicellary of a star-fish, which never has any such actual stem as in the Echinidæ.

e. Homology of the interior organs.

With regard to the other organic systems in the Brisinga: the water-system, with the exterior parts belonging thereto, (the water-feet, the madreporic body); the nervous system with its terminal apparatus of sensation; the digestive system; the blood-system; the

[*] Revision of the Echini, Part IV, pg. 668.

secretive system: the complete resemblance of all these to the same in other star-fishes, has been previously sufficiently demonstrated; for which reason it is unnecessary here again to notice each one of them separately. But with respect to the generative organs, an observation may yet not be out of place. In the arrangement of these organs, the Brisinga appears at first glance to be very remarkably distinguished from all other Asteridæ; as the generative organs are in the Brisinga quite separated from the disc, and limited to the arms only; while in all other star-fishes they take their origin from the disc itself, even if in some few forms they also extend more or less into the cavities of the arms. This apparently very anomalous case may yet be quite naturally attributed to the excessive reduction of the disc in the Brisinga, which only corresponds to the central part of the disc in other star-fishes; while the peripheral part of the disc in these, is in reality homologous with the basal part of the arms in the Brisinga. If we admit this, it will easily appear that the organs of generation (as described in the Brisinga coronata) really correspond, not only in structure but also in position, to what is normal in star-fishes generally (comp. moreover the 2 schematic figures 36 and 37 in Tab. VI).

6.

Relation of the genus Brisinga to now living star-fishes.

Among the now living star-fishes, the genus Brisinga seems indeed to stand rather isolated, as well with regard to its exterior habitus as in respect of particular points of its interior organisation. There are however certain genera of star-fishes with which it seems to exhibit a closer affinity than with others. Among the better known native genera, there are chiefly 2 which we may take as instances of this, namely Asterias and Solaster. The former is, next to the Brisinga, that one of all our Asteridæ in which the disc is the most reduced relatively to the arms; and it is probably also, next to the Brisinga, that one which we must regard as the oldest or least altered star-fish form, a conclusion which is completely corroborated by paleontological indications. The Brisinga shews affinity to the genus Asterias in the form of its pedicellariæ, partly also in the structure of the cuticular skeleton, and finally in the more solid composition of the interior set of vertebræ (the oral ring). The genus Asterias has however 4 rows of water-feet; while the Brisinga has only 2, in this respect resembling the genus Pedicellaster, which was established by my Father, and which in other respects is in close affinity with the genus Asterias. The Brisinga is however distinguished both from the Pedicellaster and Asterias (at least from our native species) by its considerable number of arms or rays, in which respect again it agrees better with the genus Solaster. Still neither of these genera exhibits a disc reduced in any thing like the same degree as that of the Brisinga; and even in those species of the genera Asterias (A. glacialis) and Pedicellaster which are furnished with a relatively very small disc, we shall yet find that a rather considerable number of vertebræ have entered into the formation of the disc; while the number of such vertebræ belonging to the disc in the Brisinga is properly speaking zero. It is this which properly determines the peculiar exterior habitus, so different from that of other known star-fishes, that distinguishes the genus Brisinga, and gives to it at first glance a certain habitual similarity to the Ophiuræ.

7.

Relation of the genus Brisinga to extinct star-fishes.

Asbjornsen has already (l. c.) drawn attention to the habitual conformity of the genus Brisinga with the oldest known fossil star-fish Protaster. The small round ophiura-like disc, with the sharply defined arms issuing from it, in the Protaster, reminds us decidedly of the Brisinga; as also the skeleton of the arms, by its shape and composition of ambulacral and adambulacral plates only, exhibits in both forms considerable resemblance. We shall however find, on more minute examination, that the body even in this ancient form, is already considerably more centralised than in the Brisinga: a considerably greater number of vertebræ enters into the composition of the disc, notwithstanding its small dimensions. On the whole we shall find in the Protaster evident indications of the course of development diverging from the star-fish type and tending towards the Ophiuræ type, which is by no means the case in the Brisinga. Antecedently to this divergent development we must naturally presuppose a number of more indifferent stages, wherein the nature of the development would not yet be clearly indicated, in other words, wherein the cormus would shew a slighter degree of centralisation: and these stages must certainly be supposed to have been in some degree more corresponding to the Brisinga. If we admit the theory above noticed as to the composite individuality of star-fishes, or their original value as colonies of worm-like persons, we have actually in the now living Brisinga a still more primitive form than even in the Protaster, wherein this colony has already attained to a considerable degree of centralisation, and in which the number of persons (arms) has become permanently the typical number for the Echinoderms, namely 5. The Brisinga may henceforward be assumed to exhibit a still greater conformity with the supposed ancestors of the genus Protaster than with this genus itself. In any case we must consider the genus Brisinga, in respect of the general composition of the body, as the most primitive and therefore the oldest of all Echinoderms.

8.
Comparison of the 2 species of Brisinga.

The two hitherto known species of the genus Brisinga, Br. endecacnemos and Br. coronata, stand in close connexion, but exhibit nevertheless certain distinctive characteristics which make their specific distinction necessary. The latter of these species has already been exhaustively described in the foregoing pages. As regards the first species discovered, Br. endecacnemos, its general appearance and structure are pretty well known from Asbjörnsen's description and figures. It might possibly however not be without interest here to notice again this species, and to compare it with the Br. coronata. I have therefore added a plate (Tab. VII) in illustration; and will now briefly point out the characteristics wherein the two species differ from each other.

In size, color and general habitus they are (see Tab. VII, fig. 1) nearly similar. But an important distinctive characteristic is the number of the arms or rays. While this number is in the Br. coronata, as previously noticed, extremely variable, the number of rays in the Br. endecacnemos has already become completely permanent, and is constantly 11. In no single one of the numerous specimens which have been examined of this species, (and their number far exceeds that of the specimens taken of the other species), has there ever been noticed any deviation from this rule; for which reason also the specific denomination Endecacnemos is fully justified. The manner in which the arms are inserted on the disc is completely similar in both species. Still the interval between the bases of the arms is in the Br. endecacnemos still more restricted; so that the arms nearly touch each other at the base; while we always find in the Br. coronata an evident, even if only a small interval.

The disc is, viewed from above (see fig. 1) in both species circular; seen from the side (fig. 2) it appears however in the Br. endecacnemos somewhat higher than in the other species, and has its exterior border more perpendicular. The disc-spines, (fig. 6) are nearly similar to those in the Brisinga coronata. They stand usually still more closely together; and the proper calcareous spine exhibits at the extremity only a few secondary spines. The shape of the madreporic body (see fig. 1, 2 & 4) is characteristic for the Br. endecacnemos. It is always remarkably prominent; so that when the disc is viewed in profile (fig. 2) it projects frequently like a more than semiglobular, or even like a nearly pyramidal tubercle. On closer inspection it will be found (see fig. 4) to consist as it were of 2 parts; only the exterior, more salient part having the meandric furrows; while the other part is covered with strong pointed spines, which also (in annular arrangements) encircle the more salient part. The secretory pore situated on the dorsal side of the disc (the so-called anal aperture) has the same somewhat excentric position as in the Br. coronata; and the disc exhibits at this point a slight elevation (see fig. 2). I have not succeeded in discovering any traces of pedicellaries on the dorsal side of the disc, where in the Br. coronata they are always plainly apparent. The spines attached to the underside of the disc seem also to be somewhat different from those of the Br. coronata. The furrow-spines on the lower side of the adambulacral plates (see fig. 2, 3 & 5) are remarkably large, usually 12 for each interradial space, of which 4 especially, on the interior adambulacral plate, are remarkably long and strong, and directed inwards towards the oral aperture, whereby they appear to have assumed the functions of the proper oral spines. These latter, 6 in number, are however here (see fig. 9) extremely small and quite covered by the other spines; so that they do not become apparent until the others are removed. The oral membrane resembles completely that of the Br. coronata (see fig. 5) but is in most captured individuals difficult to perceive; as usually the folds of the stomach are evaginated a long way out of the mouth, and the oral aperture itself strongly enlarged (see fig. 3).

The arms (see fig. 1) have about the same length in proportion to the diameter of the disc, and exhibit in their general form a great resemblance to those of the Br. coronata, but are immediately distinguished by the absence of the elevated spines in annular arrangement on the transversal ribs, which are so characteristic of the latter species. Likewise we do not usually find any trace of the soft transverse ridges covered with pedicellaries, which are so distinctly marked in the Br. coronata. Only in a few unusually large specimens (see fig. 1) I have found slight indications of such ridges between the interior calcareous ribs; while in the exterior part of the arm no such indications were apparent. With respect to the calcareous ribs, they have in the Br. endocracnemos a relatively far greater extension on the arms than in the Br. coronata, being apparent on all the interior half. Their number is therefore also much greater, namely 30—40, or about twice as great as in the Br. coronata. In their shape and arrangement they correspond otherwise perfectly to those of other species; and also in this they appear frequently variously sinuous and anastomosing with each other. If we now examine these calcareous ribs with sufficient magnifying power, we shall find on them, besides numerous pedicellaries, also a single row of extremely small spines (see fig. 15). These spines are (fig. 14) compressed, lancet-formed, and, as it appears, entirely without any cuticular sheath; neither do they appear to be movably articulated to the calcareous rib, like those of the Br. coronata in the same place, but merely to represent simple processes of the same. The whole dorsal cuticle of the arms between the ribs will also be found covered with similar, although somewhat longer and thinner, small microscopic spines — quite in contrast to what is the case in the Br. coronata — whereby the surface of the arms acquires a peculiar rough, or, as it were, finely chagrined quality (see fig. 11). In the interior, at the base of the arms, these spines stand most closely; further out on the arms they are arranged in larger irregular spaces, mostly in a transverse direction and with bare intervals. All these minute spines, of which there is no trace to be seen in the Br. coronata, rise (see fig. 12) from small thin circular perforated calcareous plates in the skin; and among these spiniferous plates there are besides a great number of still smaller disc-like plates, which are without spines, but from which spines are no doubt subsequently gradually developed. By these innumerable small cuticular plates in connexion with the numerous calcareous ribs, the cuticle of the arm in the Br. endecacnemos acquires, on the whole, a considerably firmer consistency than in the Br. coronata; a fact which stands in the closest connexion with the very different arrangement of certain internal parts (the organs of generation) in the latter species, as will be further noticed in the sequel. With regard to the proper arm-spines, they are nearly like those of the Br. coronata. They are proportionally even somewhat longer than in this species, especially the so-called exterior furrow-spines which are attached in the middle of the adambulacral plates (comp. fig. 11). The number of the interior furrow-spines is moreover also rather variable in different individuals, and seems usually to increase with age. The marginal spines are in the basal part of the arm very small; but outwards they increase rapidly in length; so that in the middle of the arm they become 3 times as long as its transverse diameter. They are also movably articulated to the outer extremities of the calcareous ribs, which form very distinct plate-shaped enlargements furnished with an evident joint (see fig. 13); in the exterior part of the arm, where the calcareous ribs are wanting, they are attached to special small plates (dorsal marginal plates). At the point of the arm there is an organ of sense quite like that in the Br. coronata, and likewise arched over by a peculiar calcareous plate furnished with long marginal spines (see fig. 17).

In quite young specimens the disc (see fig. 10) is very thin and transparent; and the exterior set of vertebræ come forward here in the same manner as in equally small specimens of Br. coronata. Of the dorsal spines, a great many have still the peculiar bristle-like form which is described in the young of the Br. coronata, and which in all probability is a remnant from the embryonic or larva-state. On the other hand the madreporic body already shews completely the form and arrangements which are characteristic of the species. The arms are, in proportion to the diameter of the disc, considerably shorter than in adult specimens, evenly tapering from the very base, and as yet without any evident calcareous ribs.

In the structure of the ambulacral skeleton there is certainly a great resemblance to the Br. coronata, nevertheless, on a more minute investigation, it will be easy to discover, even here, several specific differences.

The oral ring (fig. 7) is, in conformity with the greater height of the disc, of a somewhat different shape from that of the Br. coronata, with a more sharply projecting dorsal ridge and more vertical exterior sides. The vertebræ of the exterior set are considerably shorter above and nearly disc-like; so that, when the oral ring is viewed from above, (fig. 7) they appear like an extremely narrow rim around the strongly developed interior set of vertebræ. As a consequence of this, the wedge-plates (see fig. 8) rise also more perpendicularly than in the other species. Their upper enlarged end is less tubercularly salient, and regularly formed; and the dorsal marginal plates attached to their lower extremities, stand so closely together that their exterior articulating surfaces nearly touch each other. The very narrow, scarcely perceptible, fissure between the parietal plates in the interior wall of the oral ring of the Br. coronata, is here (see fig. 7) widely gaping and spanned over with extended soft brownish ligaments. On closer comparison of the single calcareous plates which compose the oral ring, with the corresponding plates in the Br. coronata, there will likewise be found several points of dissimilarity in shape, on which however it would not be expedient here to enter. The greatest difference appears to be in the interior adambulacral plates. They are here (see fig. 9) much narrower, and have a very conspicuous instriction in the vicinity of the adoral extremity, which is thus divided, as it were, by a furrow of demarcation, from the rest of the adambulacral plate.

With regard to the ambulacral skeleton of the arms (fig. 15 & 16), the individual joints or vertebræ are on the whole shorter and broader than in the Br. coronata, especially the interior ones; and their dorsal ridge is more regularly semicylindrical: not, as in Br. coronata, distinctly enlarged at the extremities. Of the dorsal marginal plates there are always 3 distinctly developed, and rudiments of 1 or 2 others (see fig. 11, 15, 16). It is still more clearly to be seen here than in the Br. coronata, that the marginal plates further out on the arm are in reality represented by the enlarged extremities of the calcareous ribs (see fig. 11 & 13).

As to the internal organisation, we must further notice a remarkable difference between the two species of Brisinga. This remark applies to the organs of generation. While in the Br. coronata they only form 2 widely ramified symmetrical organs situated in the basal part of each arm, each organ with its single issue, they represent in the Br. endecacnemos (fig. 18 & 21) a great number of separate glandulous bodies, which are arranged on each side of the medial line in a single row, extending to about half the length of the arm. Each of these bodies has its separate issue, opening nearer to the dorsal side of the arms in a fine pore. Therefore, instead of the 2 symmetrical apertures of generation in the Br. coronata, we find here for each arm a double row of numerous apertures, as has already been remarked by Asbjörnsen. This wonderful arrangement of the generative apparatus, to which nothing corresponding is found in other star-fishes, is in so far of great interest, as we may see herein a characteristic of very ancient origin, an inheritance from the worm-like ancestors of the Brisinga, which has still been only partially preserved in the class of Crinoidæ. The ovaries (see fig. 18, 19, 20) are very slightly ramified, and often appear like

13

perfectly simple, oval, stemmed vesicles, in the interior of which the reddish yellow ova are shining. Only nearer to the base of the arm, they exhibit in large specimens some few short and broad lobes (fig. 20). The spermaries (fig. 21, 22) are more ramified, and look like small bunches of grapes, with considerably smaller rounded lobes of a whitish color.

The color of the body is in both species of Brisinga tolerably uniform; but the red color of the dorsal side in the Br. endecacnemos, seems generally to be lighter or less intense than in the Br. coronata.

The remarkable difference in the occurrence of both species has been previously noticed. On our coasts it appears to be quite constant.

Br. endecacnemos was first discovered by Asbjørnsen in the interior of the Hardangerfjord, where its occurrence is not so very rare in one locality (Ilesthammer). It is found here, as in every other place, only on a rocky bottom, on the steep incline from the outside deep (100 fathoms) towards the shore. Subsequently it has also been met with in a few other places in the same fjord under similar circumstances. But on the other hand, it was not known among us as occurring elsewhere than in the Hardangerfjord, until I found it again some years ago at Floro, 12 miles north of Bergen. The figures here given are taken from the fine specimen then obtained. According to reports of the Atlantic expeditions organised by the English government, it is found at least as far towards the south as the west coast of Portugal, where several specimens were taken, partly at very considerable depths, during the Porcupine's expedition under the guidance of Mr. Jeffreys.

9.

On the systematic position of the genus Brisinga, with remarks on the classification of the star-fishes in general.

We have previously mentioned that the genus Brisinga, according to its whole organisation, is a genuine star-fish, and has nothing in common with the Ophiuræ, which latter must be considered as a diverging branch from the group of the Asteridæ, wherein the course of development has taken a very peculiar direction different from that of the star-fish now living. In the general composition of the body, and especially in the extremely slight centralisation of the cormus, the Brisinga certainly occupies a rather indifferent position; and it may in this respect be considered as more nearly agreeing with the ancient primitive forms from which all the other echinoderms have sprung. But on the other hand, the organisation is otherwise completely developed in the manner characteristic of the star-fishes; for which reason it must in a natural system be necessarily referred to them. Thus there only remains the task of assigning to it its systematic place in the order of the star-fishes.

In the division of the star-fishes it has, as is well known, been usual according to Müller & Troschel[1] to have regard chiefly to 2 characteristics, namely the arrangement of the water-feet in 2 or 4 rows, and the presence or absence of the anal aperture. To neither of these characteristics can there however in my opinion be attributed such a systematic importance, as that any natural division could be established on that basis. According to the first mentioned characteristic, the star-fishes generally are divided into 2 large groups or sub-orders: those with 4, and those with 2 rows of water-feet. To the former group there belong only a proportionally small number of forms; while the majority of known star-fishes belong to the latter group, or those with only 2 rows of water-feet. Also the genus Brisinga would, on account of its biserial water-feet, have to be classed in the last of these groups. The unnaturalness of this binary division of the star-fishes, will however on further consideration appear manifest.

We have thus in the genus Asterias not only forms with 4, but also with more rows of water-feet; and of those star-fishes provided with 2 rows of water-feet, there are several which decidedly in all other respects approach extremely nearly to those with 4 rows. Thus the genus Pedicellaster, with 2 rows of water-feet, stands so particularly near to the genus Asterias with 4 rows, that in a natural system it must even be referred to the same family. The case is similar with the 2 genera Cribrella and Stichaster, which are undoubtedly nearly related to each other, but which have been formerly, on account of the before-mentioned difference in the arrangement of the water-feet, placed in quite different sub-orders. Finally we have in the interesting form Pteraster multipes, discovered by my Father, an instance of considerable variation occurring in respect of the arrangement of the water-feet, even within the limits of one and the same generic type. This star-fish, which otherwise, as well according to its exterior habitus as according to its whole organisation, is a well defined genuine Pteraster, has for each ambulacrum 4 distinct rows of water-feet; while all other known species of this genus have only 2. According to the former method of division, this star-fish would therefore not only be separated generically from its near relatives Pt. militaris and Pt. pulvillus, but would have to be classed in a quite different sub-order, where it would stand together with forms with which it only exhibits a very distant affinity. It appears already, from this one instance, clearly enough, that the characteristic derived from the arrangement of the water-feet, must be entirely abandoned as systematic characteristic having the value formerly attributed to it.

Neither does the other characteristic, the presence or absence of an anal aperture, appear to me to be applicable as a principle of division; and that chiefly because the aperture which has been called anal, is frequently, perhaps in most cases, not an anal aperture, but only, as in the Brisinga, a more secretory pore. This seems especially to be the case

[1] System der Asteriden.

13*

in the star-fishes whose anal aperture is indicated as sub-central. But to ascribe to the presence or absense of this insignificant secretory pore, such a prominent importance as to make it the basis for the formation of larger groups, seems to me to be quite unreasonable. We are thereby forced to separate evidently related forms from each other. As an illustrative instance of this we may mention the 2 genera Archaster and Astropecten, which according to the earlier division belong to different groups of star-fishes: the former to those furnished with an anal aperture, and the latter to those without it. But these 2 genera are in reality so extraordinarily closely related, that even some species which now are usually referred to the genus Archaster (for instance A. Andromeda and A. Parelii) have been taken for genuine Astropectens, even up to the most recent times. Only after that the previously overlooked anal aperture (there undoubtedly a mere secretory pore) had been observed in these species, it has been found necessary, in regard to the formerly adopted method of division, to transfer them not only to another genus, but even to an entirely different group of star-fishes. Another distinctive characteristic has indeed been indicated for the genus Archaster, namely the structure of the water-feet; but that it is not possible from this either, to get any trustworthy mark of recognition, has lately been demonstrated by Lütken (l. c.). The 2 above-named species of the genus Archaster agree also in this respect completely with the species of the genus Astropecten.

As has been shewn, the previous division of the star-fishes is scarcely tenable any longer, being based on characteristics of very doubtful systematic value. As principles of division in a new classification of the Asterides, the structure of the ambulacral skeleton, the structure of the cuticular skeleton, and the relation of the other calcareous particles, spines and pedicellaries belonging to the skin, will chiefly have to be considered. Especially the pedicellaries seem in this respect to deserve our attention. They are entirely wanting in a great number of star-fishes; while in others (for instance the genus Hippaster) they exhibit a very peculiar structure and arrangement, totally different from what we have become acquainted with in the Brisinga.

With respect to the structure of the pedicellaries, the Brisinga exhibits most resemblance to the Asterias and Pedicellaster, which also agree with the Brisinga in some other points, and may therefore be considered as the nearest relatives of this genus among the star-fishes of the present day. Yet the genus Brisinga exhibits so many peculiarities, that it can scarcely be placed together with those two genera in one and the same family. The Brisinga must therefore in any case be considered as the type for a particular family among the Asterides. With respect to the place of this family in relation to the other families of the Asterides, if we are to follow a definite serial order consistent with the supposed phylogenetic development, it must be placed not at the end of the order of the Asterides, but at the very beginning, as representing the oldest and most primitive of all the Asterides.

10.
Diagnoses of Family, Genus and Species.

Familia: Brisingidæ.

Habitus externus Ophiuridarum, structura vero Asteridarum.

Discus minimus annulo sustentatus calcareo solido e vertebris modo adoralibus firmiter inter se conjunctis composito.

Corpus madreporiforme singulum tuberculiforme prope marginem disci dorsaliter situm.

Brachia perlonga a disco bene definita, tessellis ambulacralibus et adambulacralibus distinctis marginalibus vero obsoletis, sulcis ventralibus profundis, tentaculis magnis disciferis.

Cavitas intestinalis in brachia extensa ibiqve cæca radialia bene evoluta bifurcata et organa generationis continens.

Genus: Brisinga, Asbjørnsen.

Discus orbicularis, sat depressus supine cute coriacea dense spinigera tectus, inferne nullis angulis oralibus prominentibus sed cuticula nuda valde contractili os circumdante instructus. Porus secretorius subcentralis in cute dorsali perspicuus. Brachia numerosa semicylindrica, parte adorali in adultibus plus minusve subfusiformi apicem versus sensim attenuata, apice tenuissimo filiformi organo sensorio distincto terminato, ad basin utriuqve tessellis marginalibus duabus tribusve rudimentariis instructa, cute dorsali in parte basali costis calcareis transversis vario modo flexuosis ad intervalla firmata spinis marginalibus longissimis et ut ambulacralibus vaginis cutaceis magnis obvelatis.

Vertebra 1ma brachiorum in adultibus annulo calcareo disci firmiter adnata; tessellæ connectentes annuli inter qvamqve vertebram 3, media dorsaliter tuberculi instar prominente.

Pedicellariæ numerosissimæ forcipatæ apice fortiter dentato et in vaginis spinarum accumulatæ et in superficie dorsali brachiorum per fascias transversas plus minusve perspicuas distributæ.

Tentacula ambulacralia biserialia e sulcis ventralibus longe porrecta. Tentacula respirationis nulla.

Spec. 1: Brisinga endecacnemos, Asbjørnsen.

Brachia semper 11 costis calcareis numerosis (20–30) per dimidiam brachii longitudinem et ultra occurentibus spinulis perparvis microscopio modo visibilibus obsitis, cute dorsali inter easdem spinulis numerosis minimis aspera, fasciis pedicelligeris parum vel plane non perspicuis.

Corpus madreporiforme valde prominens, interdum fere conicum, ex parte spinulis rigidis armatum.

Pedicellariæ magnitudine inæqvali nonnullis in vaginis spinarum ceteris plus duplo majoribus et structura multo fortiore.

Organa generationis numerosa per dimidiam brachii longitudinem dispersa, seriem duplicem formantia, unoqvoqve poro externo discreto prope superficiem dorsalem instructo.

Spec. 2: Brisinga coronata, G. O. Sars.

Brachia numero valde inconstantia (9—13), costis calcareis circiter 12 in parte modo basali tertia occurrentibus, spinis altis coronam conspicuam formantibus armatis, cute dorsali inter costas nuda, fasciis vero pedicelligeris distinctissimis, semicylindricis, per totam brachii longitudinem usqve ad apicem conspicuis.

Corpus madreporiforme parum elevatum nullis spinulis armatum.

Pedicellariæ omnes eadem magnitudine, minimæ sed portentoso numero.

Organa generationis cujusqve brachii solummodo duo valde ramosa in parte basali symetrice disposita poro externo utrinqve singulo a basi circiter diametro disci remoto.

Explanation of the Plates.

Tab. I.

Fig. 1. A very young 10-armed specimen of Brisinga coronata, seen from above, natural size; on the left there appears a recently regenerated arm.

Fig. 2. The disc of the same specimen, with the base of 4 arms in their natural connexion, viewed from below, somewhat magnified.

Fig. 3. The same viewed from above: *b*, the madreporic body.

Fig. 4. The disc of a full grown 9-armed specimen viewed from above, very slightly magnified: *a*, the secretory pore; *b*, the madreporic body; *c c*, the radial spaces of the disc; *d d*, the interradial spaces, with the wedge-plate inserted in the angles of the arms; *e*, a recently regenerated arm.

Fig. 5. The same viewed from below: *c d e*, as in the preceding figure; *f*, the oral aperture strongly contracted.

Fig. 6. The same viewed from the side. The letters as in the 2 preceding figures.

Fig. 7. A piece of the dorsal skin of the disc, with the secretory pore (a) more strongly magnified.

Fig. 8. Perpendicular section of the dorsal skin of the disc, still more strongly magnified, shewing the 2 layers of the skin, the spines with their cuticular sheaths (b) and the pedicellariæ (a).

Fig. 9. A single disc-spine with the basal plate belonging to it, strongly magnified: *a*, the basal plate contained in the dorsal skin; *b*, the spine itself; *c*, its cuticular sheath.

Fig. 10—11. Various forms of dorsal spines.

Fig. 12. An arm of a full grown specimen, viewed from the side, natural size: *a*, the left genital aperture; *b*, the dorsal marginal plates at the base.

Fig. 13. A piece of the same about in the middle of the length of the arm, viewed from the side, slightly magnified: *1*, marginal spine; *2*, *3*, furrow-spines.

Fig. 14. The same piece viewed from below. The water-feet are removed, with exception only of 2 pairs: *1*, marginal spine; *2*, *3*, *4*, furrow-spines; *a*, water-feet.

Fig. 15. A marginal spine, magnified, and treated with a solution of potash, whereby the cuticular sheath has been rendered transparent.

Fig. 16. One of the exterior furrow-spines with its cuticular sheath.

Fig. 17. The point of the calcareous spine itself, strongly magnified.

Fig. 18, 19. Interior furrow-spines.

Fig. 20, 21. 2 of the furrow-spines of the disc.

Fig. 22. A water-foot magnified, shewing the numerous muscular fibres crossing each other.

Tab. II.

Fig. 1. A full grown 10-armed specimen of Br. coronata, viewed from above, natural size; only one of the arms drawn.

Fig. 2. An other specimen with 12 arms, of which 2 are drawn; one recently regenerated and still without evident calcareous ribs.

Fig. 3. The extremity of a monstrously developed bifurcated arm, viewed from above, natural size.

Fig. 4. The basal part of an arm, with strongly projecting calcareous ribs, and unusually numerous and interrupted bands of pedicellaries, natural size.

Fig. 5. The extremity of an arm viewed from the side, strongly magnified, shewing the dorsal bands of pedicellaries (*a*) the terminal organ of sense (*c*) and the peculiar plate (*b*) which shelters it.

Fig. 6. The same seen from below: *b, c,* as in the preceding figure.

Fig. 7. The terminal organ of sense, still more strongly magnified, seen from the side: *b,* the 2 exterior rudimentary water-feet.

Fig. 8. The disc of a full grown 11-armed specimen seen from above, slightly magnified. The dorsal skin is cut open round the periphery and turned back, in order to shew the subjacent interior organs: *a,* the madreporic body; *b,* the dorsal skin turned back; *c c,* the basal trunks of the radial cæca (to the right a bifurcation of one these indicated); *d,* the peripheral part of the stomach; *e,* the upper vault of the stomach, with its radial folds; *f,* the apparatus of secretion; *g,* section of excretory duct for the same; *h,* the porus secretorius which perforates the dorsal skin.

Fig. 9. A piece of the peripheral part of the stomach viewed from within, shewing the numerous sinuous longitudinal folds: *a,* tendinous fibres whereby this part is attached to the oral ring; *b,* the oral membrane.

Fig. 10. The upper vault of the stomach viewed from the under or interior side, shewing the numerous papillæ issuing from the same, and the terminal trunks of the radial cæca proceeding from the periphery.

Fig. 11. The disc of another likewise 11-armed specimen seen from above, after that the dorsal skin and all the interior organs situated in the cavity of the disc have been removed, whereby the skeleton (the oral ring), with its tendinous lining membrane, is entirely exposed: *a*, the madreporic body, with the sheath proceding downwards from the same, in which the so-called „heart" is inclosed; *b*, the oral membrane; *c c*, the fan-like extended tendinous fibres issuing from the upper border of the oral ring and attaching the peripheral part of the stomach; *d d*, glandulous corpuscules attached to the periphery of the circular ambulacral vessel; *e*, the oral aperture.

Fig. 12. A piece of the oral ring with the tendinous membrane that lines the same, viewed from the interior side: *a*, the madreporic body; *b*, the oral membrane; *c*, the tendinous sheath in which the „heart" is inclosed; *d d*, the glandulous corpuscules attached in the periphery of the circular ambulacral vessel; *e*, the stone canal.

Fig. 13. Some of the granulous contents of the corpuscules (d), strongly magnified.

Fig. 14. One of the glandulous corpuscules isolated.

Tab. III.

Fig. 1. Part of the disc from the side, magnified, shewing the articulating surfaces for an arm and the adjacent parts: *a*, section of the radial nerve with the blood-sinus above it; *b*, section of the radial ambulacral vessel; *c*, ampullæ for the exterior water-feet of the disc; *d*, section of one of the radial cæca

Fig. 2. Part of the disc viewed from below. The spines and the water-feet are for the greater part removed, in order to show the arrangement of the nervous system: *a a*, the radial nerves; *b b*, the circular commissure of the nerves (see also Tab. VI, fig. 1).

Fig. 3. Transverse section of the basal part of an arm of a full grown female specimen: *a*, the water-feet; *b*, vertebra; *c c*, the ampullæ for the water-feet, projecting into the cavity of the arm; *d d*, section of the 2 branches of the radial cæca; *e e*, section of the ovaries; *f f*, marginal spines.

Fig. 4. The basal part of an arm of a full grown female viewed from above, a little magnified. The dorsal skin is cut along the middle and extended on each side, to expose the strongly ramified ovaries situated in the cavity of the arm Along the middle, the skeleton of the arms appears; and on each side of it, we see the ampullæ for the water-feet arranged in pairs.

Fig. 5. An ovary of more compact form, isolated and viewed from the interior side.

Fig. 6. The same viewed from the exterior side: *a*, a piece of the skin of the arm, with the exterior genital aperture (b) situated in the same.

Fig. 7. A branch of an ovary, with (terminal) ramified cylindrical cæca.

Fig. 8. Another branch, on which the terminal cæca only form small vesicular enlargements.

Fig. 9. An ovary of a very young specimen, viewed from the exterior side, strongly magnified.

Fig. 10. The same viewed from the interior side.

Fig. 11. A terminal ramification of an ovary drawn from a fresh living specimen. Inside of the half-transparent ovarial cuticle, there appear numerous egg-cells in different stages of development.

Fig. 12—15. Egg-cells in different stages of development, with an evident germinal vesicle.

Fig. 16. A fully developed egg, in which the germinal vesicle is not visible; the yellowish red mass of yolk is surrounded by a thick pellucid chorion.

Fig. 17. The basal part of an arm of a full grown male specimen, viewed from above. The dorsal skin is, as in fig. 4, cut along the middle and extended on the sides, in order to expose the strongly developed seminaries.

Fig. 18. A seminary of a younger specimen, isolated, viewed from the interior side.

Fig. 19. The same, seen from the exterior side. a, the genital aperture.

Fig. 20. A branch of the same seminary, isolated.

Fig. 21. The extremity of a branch of a fully developed seminary, drawn from a fresh living specimen.

Fig. 22. Some of the developing cells of the spermatozoa, strongly magnified.

Fig. 23. A fascicle of fully developed spermatozoa.

Fig. 24. 3 spermatozoa isolated, very strongly magnified.

Fig. 25. An arm of a fully developed female specimen, viewed from the lower side. The skeleton of the arm, together with the parts in connexion, has been removed, in order to shew the organs lying above it in the cavity of the arm in their natural position: a a a, the radial cæca with their 2 branches; b b, the ovaries; c c, the 2 genital apertures situated symmetrically.

Tab. IV.

Fig. 1. The skeleton of the disc (the oral ring) of a fully developed 10-armed specimen, seen from above, slightly magnified; a a, the radial spaces; b b, the interradial spaces; c, oral spines.

Fig. 2. The same viewed from below.

Fig. 3. The same viewed from the side.

Fig. 4. A piece of the oral ring, more strongly magnified, seen from above.

Fig. 5. The same seen from below.

Fig. 6. The same viewed from the exterior side.

Fig. 7. The same viewed from the interior side.

Fig. 8. The same viewed obliquely from above and from the interior side, the better to see the furrow for the circular ambulacral vessel, with one of the holes through which the ambulacral vessel passes.

Fig. 9. A piece of the oral ring, from which the exterior set of vertebræ are removed.

Fig. 10. Transverse section of the oral ring in the middle of a radial space.

Fig. 11. Transverse section of the oral ring in the middle of an interradial space.

The following indications serve for the last 8 figures:

a^1, interior ambulacral plates.

a^2, exterior ambulacral plates.

ad^1, interior adambulacral plates.

ad^2, exterior adambulacral plates.

f, furrow for the radial ambulacral vessel.

k, wedge-plates.

l, interior cavity bounded by the wedge-plates and the parietal plates.

m, parietal plates.

o^1, apertures for the interior water-feet of the disc.

o^2, apertures for the exterior water-feet of the disc.

r, dorsal marginal plates.

s, furrow for the circular ambulacral vessel.

y, the circular rim, projecting from the interior wall of the oral ring, which below forms a boundary for the circular ambulacral vessel.

Fig. 12. A wedge-plate isolated, viewed from the exterior side.

Fig. 13. The same, viewed from the interior side.

Fig. 14. The same, viewed in profile.

Fig. 15. The base of the skeleton of an arm, viewed from above, somewhat magnified: $a\,a$, the dorsal ridge formed by the interior part of the ambulacral plates; $b\,b$, the lateral parts of the ambulacral plates; ad, adambulacral plates; c, the 2 connate dorsal marginal plates at the base of the arm; r, rudimentary marginal plates for attachment of marginal spines; o, holes for the water-feet.

Fig. 16. The same seen from below: f, the furrow for the ambulacral vessel; p^1, marginal spines; p^2, p^3, furrow-spines; the other letters as in the preceding figure.

Fig. 17. The same, viewed from the left side: a, ambulacral plates; ad, adambulacral plates; b, the lateral parts of the ambulacral plates; r^1, r^2, the 2 connate dorsal marginal plates at the base.

Fig. 18. Base of an ambulacral skeleton split along the middle and viewed from the surface of fracture: f, furrow for the ambulacral vessel.

14*

Fig. 19. The aboral terminal surface of an arm-vertebra: *a*, ambulacral plates; *b*, adambulacral plates: *u*, the furrow for the ambulacral vessel.

Fig. 20. The oral terminal surface of the first free arm-vertebra: *c*, dorsal marginal plates; *a, b, u*, as in the preceding figure.

Fig. 21. The extremity of the skeleton of the arm, strongly magnified, viewed from above: *a*, the terminal spine-covered calcareous plate.

Fig. 22. The same viewed from below.

Fig. 23. A complete pedicellary from the cuticular sheath of one of the oral spines, strongly magnified, viewed from the broader side. The exterior cuticular sheath has been, by means of a solution of potash, rendered transparent; so that the enclosed calcareous particles appear distinctly.

Fig. 24. The same, viewed from the narrower side.

Fig. 25. The calcareous skeleton of the same pedicellary, still more strongly magnified, viewed from the broader side: *ab*, the side pieces (*a*, the proper forceps or jaw; *b*, the lower perforated plate for insertion of the adductor-muscles); *c*, the middle piece (the articulation-plate).

Fig. 26. The same viewed from the narrower side: *m m*, the adductor-muscles; *a, b, c*, as in the preceding figure.

Fig. 27. The skeleton of a pedicellary from the cuticular sheath of one of the arm-spines, viewed from the broader side, with closed jaws.

Fig. 28. Another with widely opened jaws.

Fig. 29. The same viewed from above: for all 3 figures the indication *a, b, c*, as in figures 25 and 26.

Fig. 30. The extremities of the closed jaws, viewed from above, to shew their toothed edges.

Fig. 31. Some of the developing cells of the pedicellaries from the base of the cuticular sheath of an arm-spine.

Fig. 32—37. Pedicellary-cells in 6 different stages of development, strongly magnified.

Fig. 38. A litle young Brisinga coronata, viewed from above, natural size.

Fig. 39. The same magnified, viewed from above.

Fig. 40. A part of the same, still more strongly magnified, viewed from below: *ad'*, the 2 adambulacral plates meeting in the angle of the arms; *m*, the oral membrane; *o*, the oral aperture.

Fig. 41. Skeleton of a pedicellary from the cuticular sheath of one of the oral spines in the Brisinga endecacnemos, for comparison with fig. 25.

Fig. 42. Skeleton of one of the larger sort of pedicellaries from the cuticular sheath of one of the arm-spines of the same species, for comparison with fig. 27.

Tab. V.

Fig. 1. skeleton of the disc (the oral ring), with the base of the skeleton of 3 arms in their natural connexion, of a 9-armed specimen of Brisinga coronata, viewed from above.

Fig. 2. The same viewed from below.

Fig. 3. A complete arm-vertebra seen from above.

Fig. 4. The same viewed from the left side.

Fig. 5. The same viewed from the aboral extremity.

Fig. 6. The same viewed from below.

The following indication will serve for the 4 last figures:

      a, interior part of the ambulacral plates.

      b, lateral parts of the ambulacral plates.

      ad. the adambulacral plates.

Fig. 7. The part of the skeleton of a 9-armed specimen of Solaster endeca corresponding to fig. 1, viewed from above.

Fig. 8. A part of the same viewed from below, for comparison with fig. 2.

Fig. 9. An interradium with 2 half radii of the skeleton of Brisinga coronata represented in fig. 1.

Fig. 10. The corresponding part of the skeleton of the Solaster endeca represented in fig. 7.

In both figures the letters indicate corresponding parts:

1, 2, 3, 4, 5 ambulacral plates in their order:

ad, adambulacral plates.

c, dorsal marginal plates.

p p, parietal plates.

w, wedge-plates.

o, aperture for the passage of the radial ambulacral vessel.

s, the border of the oral ring, which below limits the furrow for the circular ambulacral vessel.

l, ligaments.

Fig. 11. A part of the skeleton of the disc (the oral ring) with the base of 3 arms of the young Br. coronata represented in Tab. IV, fig. 38—40, viewed from above, strongly magnified: *ad,* the adambulacral plates of the disc; *c,* rudimentary dorsal marginal plates: *w,* wedge-plate.

Fig. 12. The same viewed from below: *ad²,* the second pair of adambulacral plates there evidently belonging to the arms); *s,* embryonic furrow-spines: *x,* the circular rim which proceeds from the interior wall of the oral ring, and to which the oral membrane is attached.

110

Fig. 13. The oral ring of a young specimen of Br. coronata, magnified, viewed from above.

Fig. 14. Part of the same, more strongly magnified, seen from the exterior side: *w*, wedge-plate.

Fig. 15. Part of the oral ring of the same specimen, with the base of an arm in natural connexion, viewed from above: *w*, wedge-plate; *r*, dorsal marginal plates; *x*, the circular rim proceding from the interior wall of the oral ring.

Tab. V.

Fig. 1. A part of the disc (a radial space) seen from below, strongly magnified. The water-feet and the spines are removed, in order to expose the central parts of the nervous system: *a a*, the circular nerve-commissure; *b*, the radial nerve; *c*, insertion for the water-feet; *x*, a recently formed germ of an arm, on which the terminal organ of sense and the 2 rows of water-feet are already evidently traced.

Fig. 2. The part of a radial nerve belonging to the disc, together with a part of the circular commissure, isolated and viewed from the upper (interior) side: *a*, the longitudinal septum which divides the radial blood-sinus.

Fig. 3. The same viewed from the side: *a*, the septum.

Fig. 4. A piece of a radial nerve from the basal part of an arm, shewing 2 of the enlargements that correspond to the water-feet, viewed from above: *a*, the septum.

Fig. 5. Another piece with 3 enlargements viewed from below.

Fig. 6. The dorsal skin of the disc, viewed from the inner side, with the interior parts attached, chiefly to shew the complicated arrangement of the ligaments by which the stomach and the radial cæca are fixed: *a*, the secretory apparatus; *b*, the so-called „heart"; *s*, the stone-canal.

Fig. 7. The madreporic body viewed from above, magnified.

Fig. 8. The „heart" isolated and viewed from the side.

Fig. 9. A piece of the skin of the same, more strongly magnified, shewing the reticulated muscular fibres.

Fig. 10. Cells in the skin of the „heart", very strongly magnified.

Fig. 11. A recently formed germ of an arm, magnified, viewed from above: *a*, the terminal organ of sense.

Fig. 12. The same viewed from below: *a*, the terminal organ of sense: *b*, the enlargement of the radial nerve at the base of this organ; *n*, the radial nerve; *w*, rudiments of the water-feet.

Fig. 13. Another germ of an arm, treated with a solution of potash to shew the interior skeleton (s) forming itself, seen from the right side: *p*, nascent furrow-spines;

p^1, radiate calcareous bodies, forming the foundation for the terminal calcareous plate of the arm.

Fig. 14. A somewhat further developed germ of an arm, viewed from below. This preparation had been lying in maceration for a long time in a solution of potash; so that all the organic parts are quite transparent, whereby the calcareous skeleton forming itself is made to appear very distinctly: a, nascent ambulacral plates; ad, adambulacral plates; p, furrow-spines; p^1, marginal spines with rudiments of pedicellariæ; p^2, thin spines issuing from the terminal calcareous plate; b, the terminal organ of sense.

Fig. 15. The extremity of the same germ of the arm, viewed from above, to shew the formation of the cuticular skeleton: b, the terminal organ of sense; r, calcareous concretions in the dorsal skin forming the foundations for the transversal calcareous ribs; t, the growing terminal calcareous plate with its spines (p^1); p, marginal spines with nascent pedicellaries.

Fig. 16. The basal part of the skeleton of a recently formed arm, magnified, viewed from above: a, ambulacral plates; ad, adambulacral plates; r r, the 2 interior dorsal marginal plates (here distinctly separated); r^1, rudimentary marginal plates further out on the arm; p, furrow-spines; p^1, marginal spines.

Fig. 17–23. Successive development of an ambulacral plate, strongly magnified.

Fig. 24. A recently formed adambulacral plate.

Fig. 25. One of the radially ramified calcareous concrements which form the foundation of the terminal calcareous plate, strongly magnified.

Fig. 26–31. Successive development of an arm-spine.

Fig. 32. One of the thin spines attached to the terminal calcareous plate, isolated.

Fig. 32 (bis). A recently formed water-foot.

Fig. 33. A piece of the embryonal cuticular skeleton of the dorsal skin of the disc, strongly magnified.

Fig. 34. One of the echinulated spines attached to the same.

Fig. 35. Schematic representation of the digestive system (the stomach with radial cæca) of a 10-armed specimen, viewed from above, natural size.

Fig. 36. Section of the disc, and base of an arm of Brisinga coronata (schematic figure). The section goes to the left, through an interradial space; and to the right, through a radial space. The dotted line refers to the next figure.

Fig 37. A similar section of Solaster endeca.

The following corresponding indications will serve for both figures:

> a, the furrow for the radial ambulacral vessel.
>
> g, genital organ.
>
> h, the „heart" with the stone canal.
>
> w, the madreporic body.
>
> m (bis), the oral aperture.

m, r, the oral ring.
s, secretory apparatus.
p, oral spines.
r, radial cæca.
st, stomach.

Tab. VII.

Brisinga endecacnemos.

Fig. 1. A full grown specimen viewed from above, natural size. One of the arms is completely developed; another is broken off near the middle, and the point recently regenerated; a 3ᵈ is just newly formed.

Fig. 2. The disc of the same specimen, somewhat magnified, viewed from the side.

Fig. 3. The same viewed from below. The folds of the stomach are strongly protruded; so that the oral membrane is not visible.

Fig. 4. The madreporic body, with a piece of the dorsal skin, strongly magnified, viewed from above.

Fig. 5. A piece of the disc of another specimen, viewed from below, to shew the oral membrane and the arrangement of the spines.

Fig. 6. 3 of the dorsal disc-spines, with basal plates belonging to them imbedded in the skin.

Fig. 7. The oral ring viewed from above, magnified.

Fig. 8. A piece of the same, somewhat more strongly magnified, viewed from the exterior side.

Fig. 9. The same viewed from below. The spines are removed, with exception of the rudimentary oral spines proceding from the extremity of the interior contiguous adambulacral plates.

Fig. 10. The disc of a very young specimen, viewed from above.

Fig. 11. The base of a dessicated arm, viewed from the left side, slightly magnified.

Fig. 12. Calcareous bodies and small spines from the dorsal skin of the same, strongly magnified.

Fig. 13. Extremity of one of the transversal calcareous ribs, with a marginal spine.

Fig. 14. One of the small spines situated on the calcareous ribs, strongly magnified.

Fig. 15. Base of the skeleton of the arm, viewed from above.

Fig. 16. The same viewed from below.

Fig. 17. The extremity of an arm, viewed from the left side and strongly magnified. The preparation is treated with a solution of potash; so that the interior skeleton is distinctly seen through the skin.

Fig. 18. The basal half of an arm of a full grown female, viewed from above, natural size. The dorsal skin is cut open along the middle and turned back on the sides, to expose the numerous ovaries attached along both sides.

Fig. 19. An ovary consisting only of a single cæcum, isolated.

Fig. 20. Another ovary, with incipient dichotomic division.

Fig. 21. Base of an arm of a full grown male, viewed from above. The dorsal skin is, as in the preceding preparation, cut open along the middle: its left half is removed, while the right is spread out to expose the cluster-shaped seminaries.

Fig. 22. A seminary isolated and more strongly magnified.

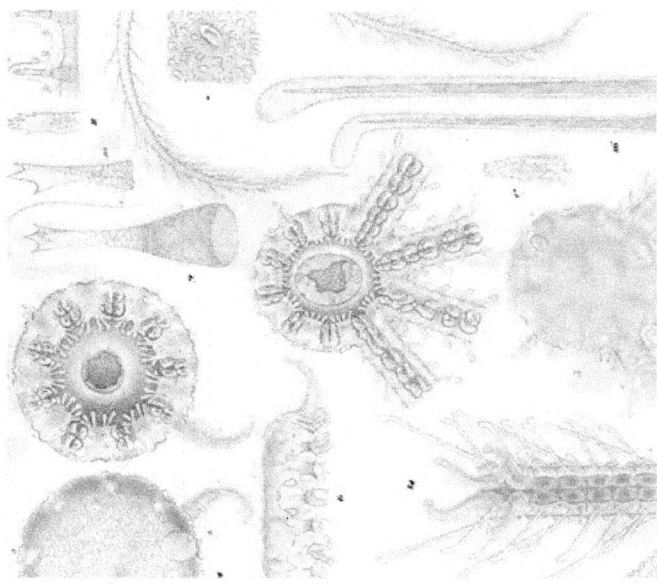

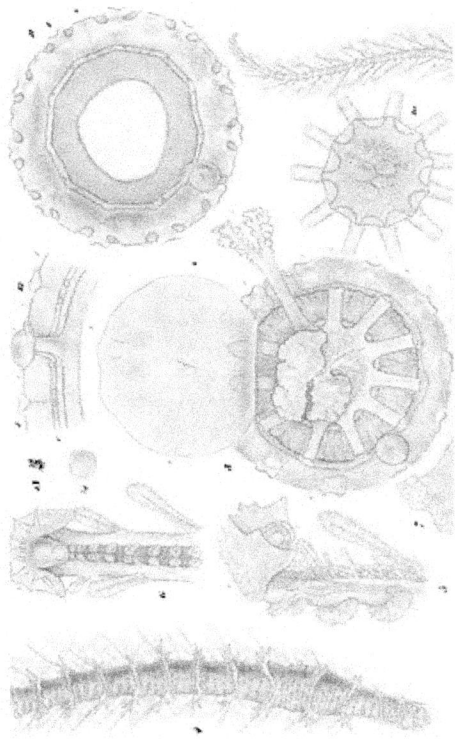

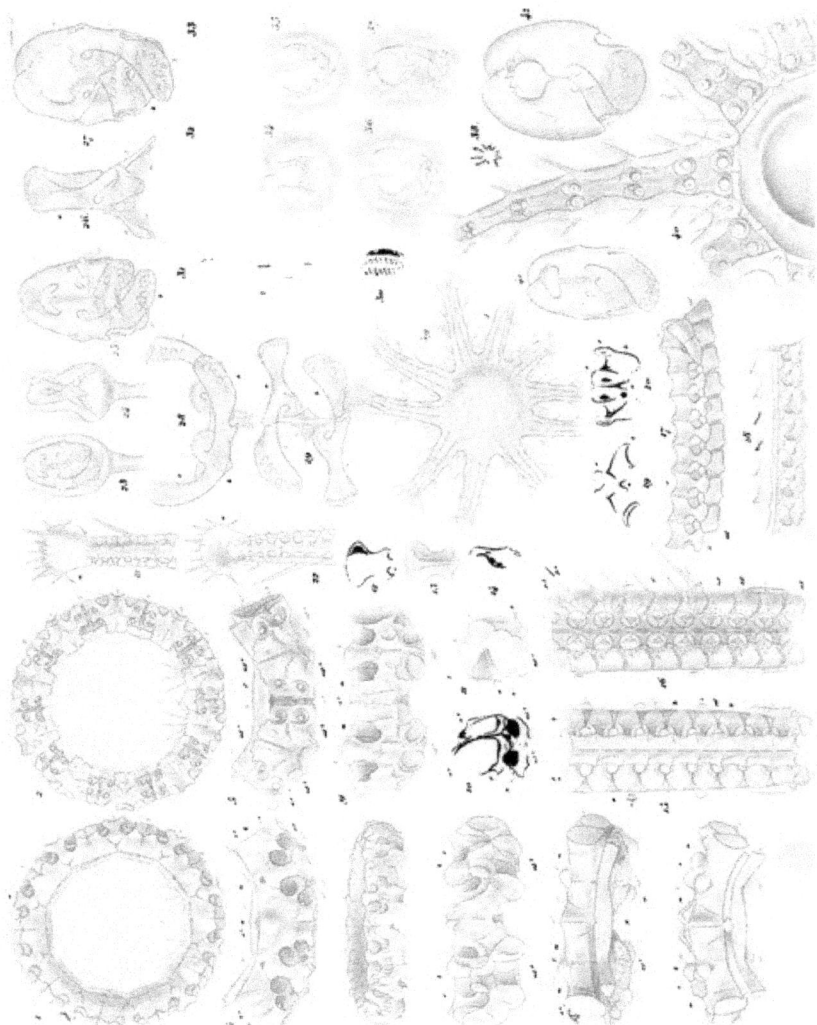

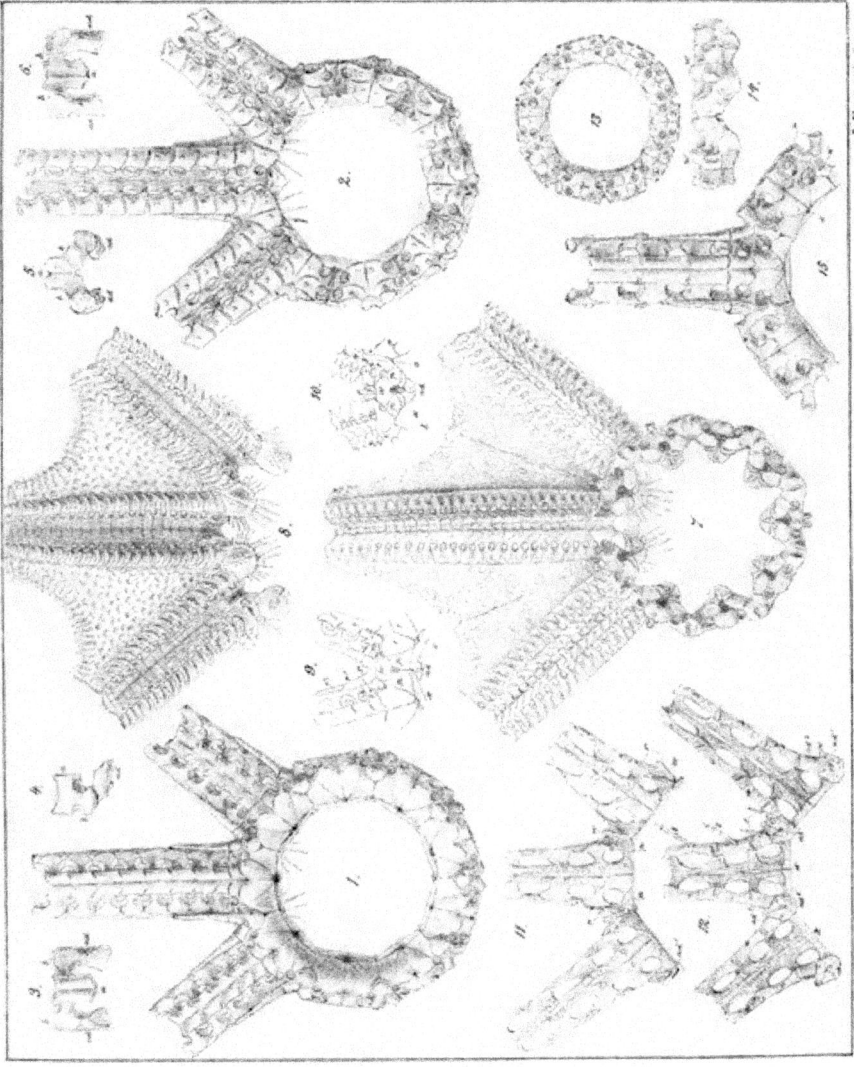

Tab. V.

G. O. Sars, udag pryels.

L. Foss? inth. Xun.

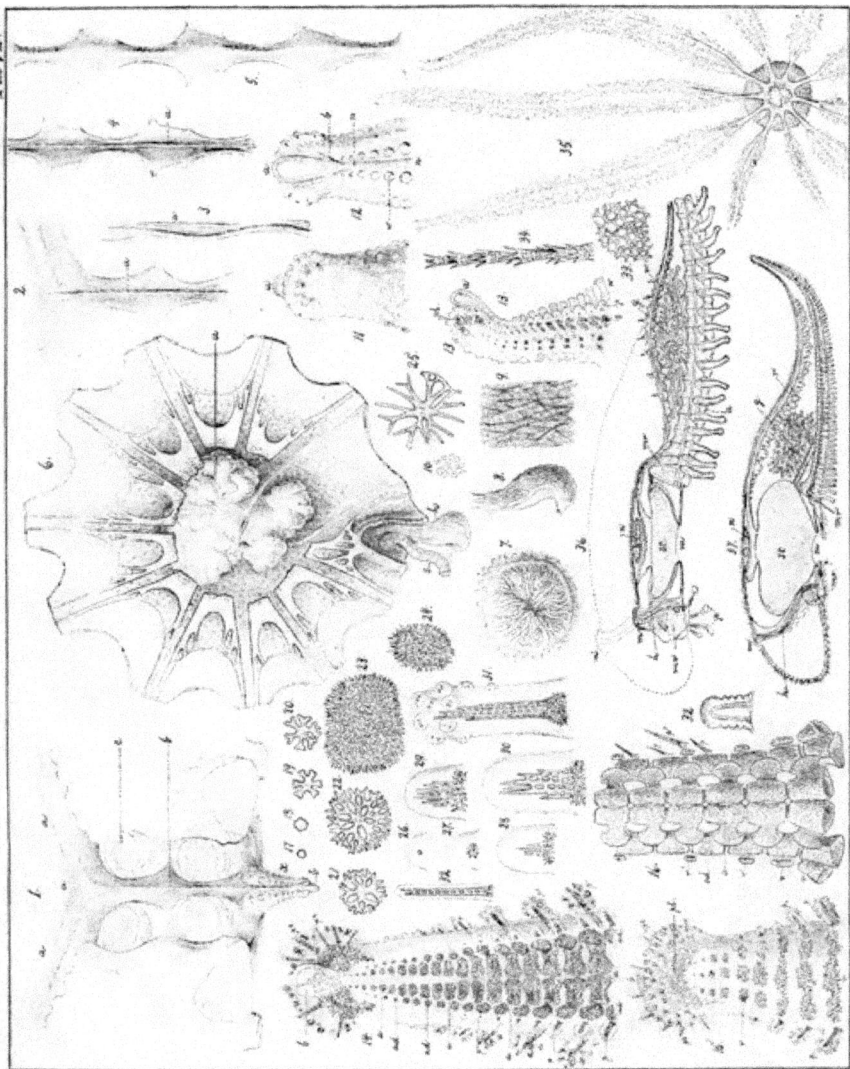

G.O.Sars autograph.

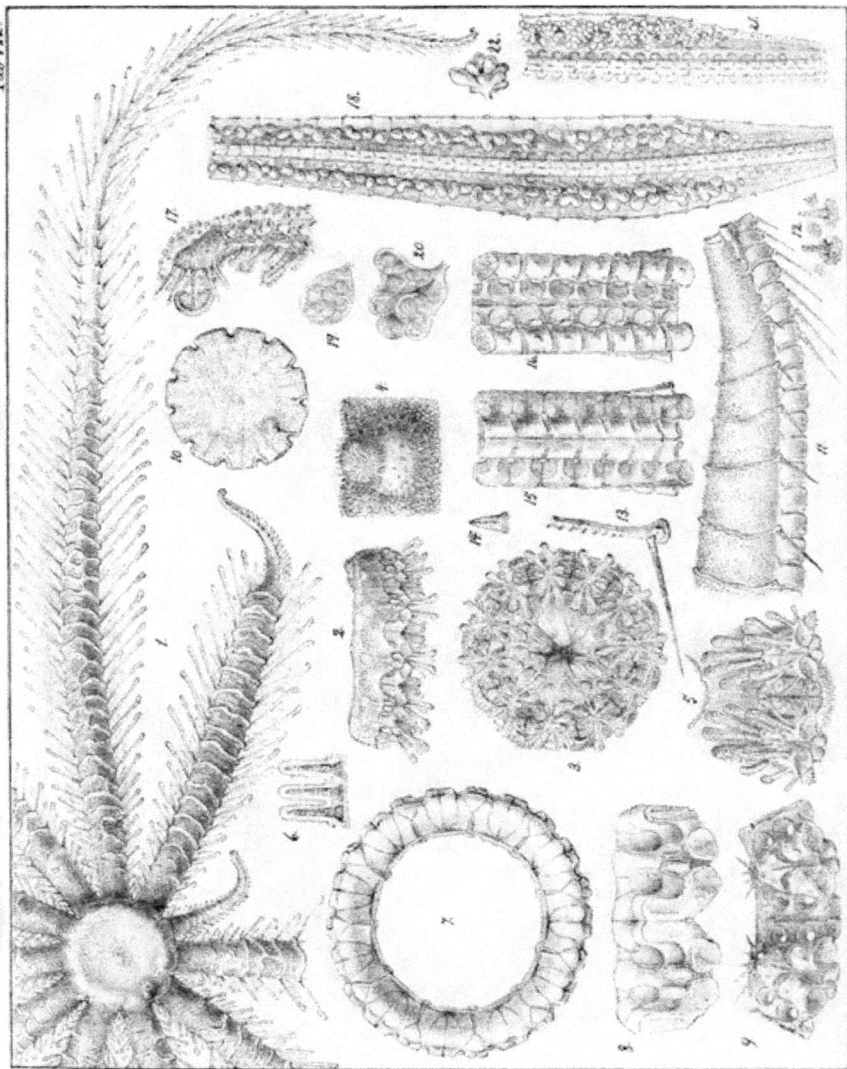

Tab VII.

L. Fehr lith. Inst.

ON

SOME REMARKABLE FORMS OF ANIMAL LIFE

FROM THE GREAT DEEPS OFF THE NORWEGIAN COAST.

(SEQUEL TO THE UNIVERSITY PROGRAM PUBLISHED UNDER THE SAME TITLE IN 1872, PARTLY FROM
POSTHUMOUS MANUSCRIPTS OF THE LATE PROFESSOR Dr. M. SARS).

II.

RESEARCHES ON THE STRUCTURE AND AFFINITY OF THE GENUS

BRISINGA,

BASED ON THE STUDY OF A NEW SPECIES:

BRISINGA CORONATA.

BY

GEORGE OSSIAN SARS,

PROFESSOR OF ZOOLOGY AT THE UNIVERSITY OF CHRISTIANIA.

WITH 4 COPPER PLATES AND 3 AUTOGRAPHIC PLATES.

(Separately Printed from the last half-year 1874.)

CHRISTIANIA.
PRINTED BY A. W. BRØGGER.

1875.

Catalogue

of the scientific works and papers published by the late Professor Dr. M. Sars.

Works published separately.

1. Bidrag til Søidyrenes Naturhistorie m. 6 Pl. Bergen. 1829.
2. Beskrivelser og Iagttagelser over nogle mærkelige eller nye i Havet ved den Bergenske Kyst levende Dyr, m. 15 Pl. Bergen 1835.
3. Fauna litteralis Norvegiæ. Part I. m. 10 Pl. Christiania 1846.
4. Fauna littoralis Norvegiæ. Part II. Bergen 1856.
5. Iagttagelser over den postpliorene eller glaciale Formation i en. Del af det sydlige Norge. Univ.-Program. Chr. 1860.
6. Om Siphonodentalium vitreum, en ny Slægt og Art af Dentalidernes Familie. m. 3 Pl. Univ.-Program. Chr. 1861.
7. Oversigt af Norges Echinodermer, m. 16 Pl. Chr. 1861.
8. Beskrivelse over Lophogaster typicus, en mærkelig Form af de lavere tiføddede Krebsdyr, m. 3 Pl. Univ.-Program. Chr. 1862.
9. Om de i Norge forekommende fossile Dyrlevninger fra Qvartærperioden, et Bidrag til vor Faunas Historie m. 4 Pl. Univ.-Program. Chr. 1865..
10. Mémoires pour servir à la connaissance des Crinoïdes vivants, avec 6 pl. Univ.-Program. Chr. 1863.

Treatises inserted in „Magazin for Naturvidenskaberne."

11. Zoologiske Iagttagelser m. 1 Pl. 1829.
12. Undersøgelser over nogle lavere Dyrs Udvikling. 1829.
13. Beretning om en i Sommeren 1849 foretagen zoologisk Reise i Lofoten og Finmarken. 1849.
14. Bemærkninger over det Adriatiske Havs Fauna sammenlignet med Nordhavet. 1853.
15. Bidrag til Kundskaben om Middelhavets Littoral-Fauna I. m. 2 Pl. 1856.
16. Bidrag til Kundskaben om Middelhavets Littoral-Fauna II. m. 2 Pl.
17. Beretning om en i Sommeren 1859 foretagen zoologisk Reise ved Kysten af Romsdals Amt. 1861.
18. Beretning om en i Sommeren 1860 foretagen Reise i en Del af Christiania Stift for at undersøge de i den saakaldte Glacialformation forekommende organiske Levninger. 1862.
19. Indberetning om en i Sommeren 1861 foretagen Reise i en Del af Christiania Stift for at fortsætte Undersøgelserne af de i vor Glacialformation indeholdte organiske Levninger. 1863.
20. Geologiske og zoologiske Iagttagelser, anstillede paa en Reise i en Del af Throndhjems Stift i Sommeren 1862. 1863.
21. Bidrag til Kundskab om Christianiafjordens Fauna I m. 7 Pl. 1868.

Treatises inserted in „Wiegmann's Archiv für Naturgeschichte."

22. Beitrag zur Entwickelungsgeschichte der Mollusken und Zoophyten, m. 2 Pl. 1840.
23. Ueber die Entwickelung der Medusa aurita und Cyanea capillata. m. 1 Pl. 1841.
24. Ueber die Entwickelung der Seesterne, m. 1 Pl. 1841.
25. Ueber einen Eingeweidewurm in einer Aalephe. 1845.
26. Zusätze zu die von mir gegebenen Darstellung der Entwickelung der Nudibranchien. 1845.
27. Ueber die Entwickelung der Juogen bei einer Annelide und über die äussere Unterschiede zwischen beiden Geschlechtern. 1845.

Papers read at the meetings of the Scandinavian naturalists.

7th meeting in Christiania 1856.

28. Om 5 nye Krebsdyr.
29. Om Anthocalerces Duchenii.
30. Om Søliljernes Udvikling.
31. Om nogle Hydroider.
32. Bemærkninger over Brisinga endecacnemos.
33. Om Comatula Sarsi. i Pentacrinustilstand.
34. Om Medusernes Udvikling.

8th meeting in Copenhagen 1860

35. Om nogle nye Echinodermer fra den norske Kyst.
36. Om Siphonodentalium vitreum.
37. Om en Del norske Annelider.
38. Om nogle norske Coelenterater.

Catalogue

of the scientific works and papers published by G. O. Sars.

Works published separately.

rekommende Mysider. Part. II., m. 3. Pl.
Christiania 1872.
7. On some remarkable forms of animal life
from the great deeps of the Norwegian coast.
I. (partly from posthumous manuscripts of

the late Professor M. Sars) f. w. 6 pl. University-Program. Chr. 1872.
8. Indberetninger til Departementet for det Indre om de i Aarene 1870—73 anstillede
fortsatte Undersøgelser over Saltvandsfiske-
rierne. m. 2 Karter. Chr. 1874.

Treatises inserted in „Nyt Magazin for Naturvidenskaberne.“

9. Beretning om en i Sommeren 1862 foretagen zoologisk Reise i Christianias og Trond-
hjems Stifter. 1863.
10. Beretning om en i Sommeren 1863 foretagen zoologisk Reise i Christiania Stift. 1864.
11. Beretning om en i Sommeren 1865 foretagen zoologisk Reise ved Kysterne af Christianias og Christianssands Stifter. 1866.
12. Undersøgelser over Christianiafjordens Dyb-

randsfauna, anstillede paa en i Sommeren
1868 foretagen zoologisk Reise. 1869.
13. Bidrag til Kundskab om Christianiafjordens
Fauna II (Crustacea, Mollusca) m. 6 Pl.
(from posthumous manuscripts of the late
Professor M. Sars). 1870.
14. Bidrag til Kundskab om Christianiafjordens
Fauna III (Annelida) m. 5. Pl. (partly from
posthumous manuscripts of the late Professor M. Sars). 1873.

Treatises inserted in „Öfversigt af Kgl. Vetenskaps Akademiens Förhandlingar.“

15. Nya arter af Cumacea samlade under Kgl.
Svenska Korvetten Josephines Expedition
i Atlantiska Oceanen år 1869 (preliminary
rapport). 1871.
16. Cumaceer fra de store Dybder i Nordis-

havet, indsamlede ved de Svenske arktiske
Expeditioner 1861 og 1868 (preliminary
rapport). 1871.
17. Beskrivelse af nya Vestindiske Cumaceer
opdagede af Dr. A. Goës (abstract). 1871.

Treatises inserted in „Kongl. Svenska Vetenskaps Akademiens Handlinger.“

18. Beskrivelse af de paa Fregatten Josephines
Expedition fundne Cumaceer, m. 20 Pl. 1873.
19. Om Cumaceer fra de store Dybder i Nord-
ishavet m. 4 Pl. 1873.

20. Beskrivelse af nye nye Cumaceer fra Vestin-
dien og det sydatlantiske Ocean. m. 6 Pl. 1874.

Treatises inserted in „Christiania Videnskabs-Selskabs Forhandlinger.“

1861.
21. Om de i Omegnen af Christiania forekommende Cladoceer.
22. Fortsatte Bidrag til Kundskaben om de i
Christianias Omegn forekommende Cladoceer.
1862.
23. Oversigt af de indenlandske Ferskvandsco-
pepoder.
1863.
24. Om en anomal Gruppe af Isopoder.
1864.
25. Om den aberrante Krebsdyrgruppe Cumacea
og dens nordiske Arter.
1865.
26. Oversigt af Norges marine Ostracoder.
27. Om Vintertorskens (Gadus morhua) For-
plantning og Udvikling.
28. Beskrivelse af en ved Lofoten indbjerget
Rorhval (Balænoptera musculus), m. 3. Pl.
1865.
29. Om individuelle Variationer hos Røskvalerne
og de deraf betingede Uligheder i den ydre
og indre Bygning, m. 2 Tabeller.
1869.
30. Nye Dybvandscrustaceer fra Lofoten.

1871.
31. Nye Echinodermer fra den norske Kyst.
32. Diagnoser af nye Annelider fra Christiania-
fjorden (from posthumous manuscripts of
the late Professor M. Sars).
33. Undersøgelser over Hardangerfjordens Fauna
I. (Crustacea).
1872.
34. Bidrag til Kundskaben om Dyrelivet paa
vore Havbanker.
1873.
35. Om en dimorph Udvikling samt Generati-
onsvexel hos Leptodora, m. 1 Pl.
36. Bemærkninger over de til Norges Fauna
hørende Phyllopoder.
37. Bidrag til Kundskaben om Norges Hydroider, m. 4 autographiske Pl.
1874.
38. Om en hidtil lidet kjendt mærkelig Slægts-
type af Polyzoer, m. 2 autograph. Pl.
39. Om Hummerens postembryonale Udvikling,
m. 2 autogr. Pl.
1875.
40. Om Blaahvalen (Balænoptera Sibbaldii) med
Bemærkninger om nogle andre ved Fin-
markens Kyster forekommende Hvaldyr, m.
1 lith. Pl.